Discover your teaching strengths!

UNIVERSAL BEST PRACTICES FOR ALL LEARNERS

The Neurodiversity and Inclusion Learning Environments Profile (NAILEP)

ADAM D. MEYERSIECK

Universal Best Practices for All Learners

The Neurodiversity & Inclusion Learning Environments Profile (NAILEP)

First Edition

Find your NAILEP unique access link on page 5

Graphics/Layout by Adam D Meyersieck

All materials in this book and the Neurodiversity and Inclusion Learning Environments Profile (NAILEP)© not identified as being reprinted from other sources are copyrighted ©2024 by Legacy Education Group, LLC. All rights reserved. You may not distribute, copy or otherwise reproduce any portion of these materials for sale or for commercial use without written permission from Legacy Education Group, LLC and/or the Author.

ISBN: 979-8-218-47043-2

ABOUT THE DEVELOPER

Adam D. Meyersieck is an international Specialist Leader of Education in the United Kingdom and a Professor of Special Education Graduate Studies in the Educator Preparation Programs at Central Michigan University. He founded Legacy Education Group, the Islington Dyslexia Network, and led the Surrey Inclusion Outreach Service in England from its outset. He has served as a school governor, special education teacher, curriculum and assessment leader, special education coordinator, and author. He has delivered presentations and conducted workshops in the United States, Europe, Africa, and Australia, and works with schools, families, and organizations to improve understanding and quality of learning environments for students who don't "fit in the box".

Adam has written, edited, and produced numerous articles, books, and educational development and training programs, including *AI In Education: 100 Ways To use ChatGPT In The Classroom*, *Neurodiverse and Inclusive Environments: Universal Best Practices for All Learners*, the *Neurodiversity & Inclusion Learning Environments Profile*, *Multi-tiered Systems of Support: Reality or Just Another American Dream?*, and various other articles.

He has an undergraduate in Special Education from Central Michigan University and a Master of Arts in Specific Learning Disabilities (Dyslexia) from University College London's Institute of Education. He also earned the National Professional Qualification for Senior Leadership in the United Kingdom, and was named a Specialist Leader of Education by national leaders in the UK. He now works and resides in Colorado.

CONTACT
www.Legacy-Ed.com
adam@legacy-ed.com

ACKNOWLEDGMENTS

To every student, parent, and colleague who caused me to rethink, restructure, and recreate our learning environment...

This is for you.

PREFACE

"In the matter of reforming things, as distinct from deforming them, there is one plain and simple principle; a principle which will probably be called a paradox. There exists in such a case a certain institution or law, let us say, for the sake of simplicity, a fence or gate erected across a road. The more modern type of reformer goes gaily up to it and says, "I don't see the use of this; let us clear it away." To which the more intelligent type of reformer will do well to answer: "If you don't see the use of it, I certainly won't let you clear it away. Go away and think. Then, when you can come back and tell me that you do see the use of it, I may allow you to destroy it.” G.K. Chesterton

You are an Intelligent Reformer.

Here's to the crazy ones.
The misfits.
The rebels.
The troublemakers.
The round pegs in the square holes.

The ones who see things differently.

They're not fond of rules.
And they have no respect for the status quo.

You can quote them, disagree with them,
glorify or vilify them.
About the only thing you can't do is ignore them.

Because they change things.

They push the human race forward.

While some may see them as the crazy ones,
we see genius.

Because the people who are crazy enough to think
they can change the world, are the ones who do.

© 1997 Apple Computer, Inc.

CONTENTS

	Page #
How to use this program	i
Invitation: Embrace your strengths	4
Part 1: Foundations for High Quality Learning Environments	11
Part 2: The Four Key Strengths & Deep Dives	21

Deep Dives:
- Communication & Interaction (C&I) — 44
- Learning & Cognition (L&C) — 67
- Social-Emotional Strengthening (SES) — 101
- Executive Functioning (EF) — 136

Research Supporting the Four Key Strengths of High Quality Learning Environments — 164

HOW TO USE THIS PROGRAM: 7 STEPS

The following pages provide guidance on how to effectively utilize this program to identify and enhance your individual teacher strengths within your school. Here is a quick overview:

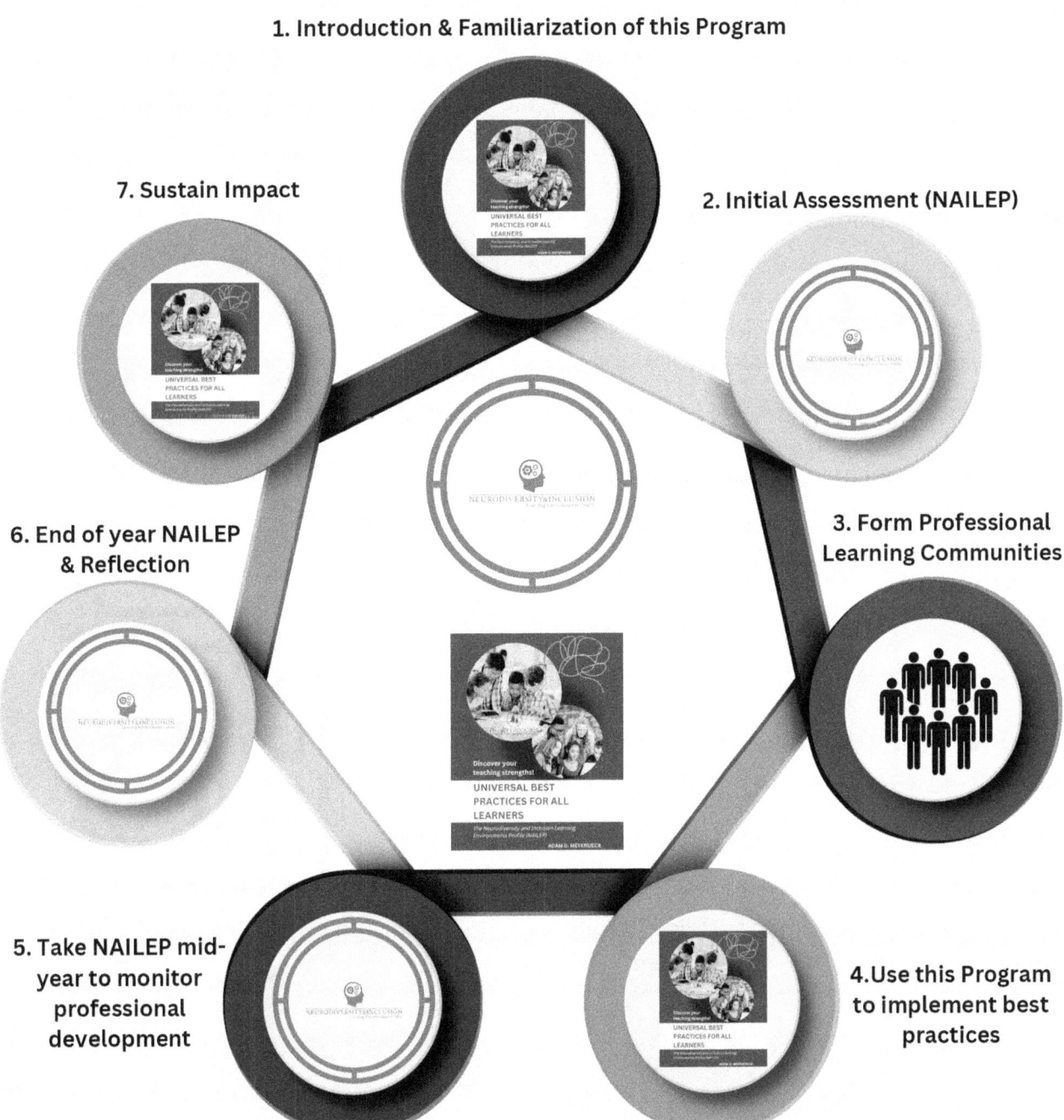

1. Introduction & Familiarization of this Program
2. Initial Assessment (NAILEP)
3. Form Professional Learning Communities
4. Use this Program to implement best practices
5. Take NAILEP mid-year to monitor professional development
6. End of year NAILEP & Reflection
7. Sustain Impact

7 STEPS TO SUCCESS

Step 1: Introduction and Familiarization

1.1. Read the Program Overview
- Start by reading through the introduction and overview sections of this program book/guide. Familiarize yourself with the four key domains: Communication and Interaction, Learning and Cognition, Social-Emotional Strengthening, and Executive Functioning.

1.2. Understand the NAILEP Tool
- The Neurodiversity & Inclusion Learning Environments Profile (NAILEP) is a key component of this program. Learn how this tool measures and analyzes strengths in your classroom environment to support all students, including those with neurodiverse needs.

Step 2: Initial Assessment

2.1. Take the Initial NAILEP Assessment
- At the beginning of the program, complete the NAILEP assessment. This will provide a baseline measurement of your strengths and areas for growth in the four key domains.

2.2. Review Your Results
- Analyze your NAILEP results to identify your strengths and areas for improvement. This will help you set specific goals for your professional development.

Step 3: Forming Professional Learning Communities (PLCs)

3.1. Identify Leaders
- Based on the NAILEP results, identify teachers who excel in each of the four domains. These teachers will act as leaders within your school's Professional Learning Communities (PLCs).

3.2. Create PLCs
- Form PLCs within your school, grouping teachers by their areas of strength. These communities will collaborate regularly to share strategies, support each other, and drive continuous improvement.

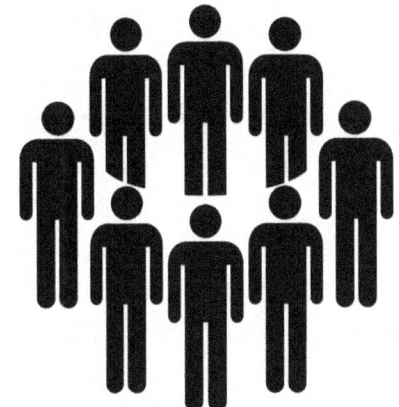

Step 4: Implementing Best Practices

4.1. Follow the Program Roadmap
- Use the book/guide to walk through the 90 key indicators of teacher strengths. Implement the recommended best practices and strategies in your classroom.

4.2. Ongoing Professional Development
- Participate in regular training sessions and workshops provided by the program. These sessions will help you develop new skills and refine your teaching practices.

Step 5: Mid-Program Assessment and Adjustment

5.1. Take the Mid-Program NAILEP Assessment
- Halfway through the program, take the NAILEP assessment again. Compare your results with your initial assessment to track your progress.

5.2. Adjust Your Strategies
- Based on your mid-program assessment results, adjust your strategies and focus areas. Continue to leverage your strengths and work on areas that need improvement.

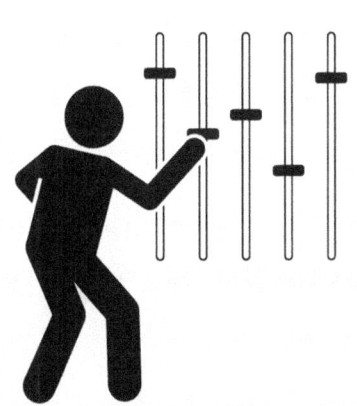

Step 6: Final Assessment and Reflection

6.1. Take the Final NAILEP Assessment
- At the end of the program, complete the NAILEP assessment one last time. This will provide a comprehensive view of your growth and development throughout the program.

6.2. Reflect on Your Journey
- Reflect on your journey and the progress you've made. Celebrate your successes and identify any remaining areas for growth.

Step 7: Sustaining the Program's Impact

7.1. Continue PLC Activities
- Maintain your Professional Learning Communities beyond the program's duration. Continue collaborating and sharing best practices to sustain the program's impact.

7.2. Ongoing Learning and Development
- Stay engaged with ongoing professional development opportunities. Keep up-to-date with the latest research and strategies in neurodiversity and inclusive education.

Additional Resources
- Visit www.legacy-ed.com for more information and support materials.
- Access online seminars, webinars, and additional reading materials to further enhance your learning experience.

By following these steps, you will be well on your way to creating an inclusive, supportive, and effective learning environment for all students.

INVITATION: EMBRACE YOUR STRENGTHS

Creating Neurodiverse & Inclusive Learning Environments for All Learners

Welcome to the **Neurodiverse & Inclusive Learning Environments Family**, an international community of dedicated professionals committed to creating optimal learning environments for all students. In this ambitious endeavor, we will strive to embrace neurodiversity and foster inclusive classrooms. As you embark on this journey, your newfound awareness and preparedness to support neurodiverse learners will set you apart. Children are entering school with challenges we have not seen at this magnitude, and many educators are struggling. Although well-meaning, trying to play "intervention catch up" is not working. Neurodivergencies present themselves through various patterns of observable and unobserved behavior, encompassing conditions such as dyslexia, dyscalculia, ADHD, speech and language impairment, autism spectrum disorder (ASD), motor skills difficulties, processing challenges, and more. Acknowledging the vast array of these differences, we understand that it is impossible for any single person to cater to the specific needs of every student. The expectation to adapt and simplify lessons for all, while maintaining standardized test performance, has led to burnout among many dedicated teachers. This program aims to help prevent that by equipping you with the tools and strategies needed to thrive in your role as a leader of education.

Along with this book, you now also have access to the Neurodiversity & Inclusion Learning Environments Profile (NAILEP) to determine teacher strengths in your school. Learn more at www.legacy-ed.com.

THE NEURODIVERSITY & INCLUSION LEARNING ENVIRONMENTS PROFILE (NAILEP)

The **Neurodiversity and Inclusion Learning Environments Profile (NAILEP)©** is an online individual and school profile measure that provides a strengths analysis of your classroom learning environment for supporting and strengthening all students, including those with learning differences. The NAILEP is suitable for ambitious teachers and school leaders who wish to create learning environments where all students can thrive.

How well does your learning environment support all learners, including those with neurodivergent needs?

The NAILEP is a professional growth measure that explores four key areas of practice that can affect neurodiverse learners' ability to thrive in your school or learning environment, including strategies in your environment to support:

- Communication & Interaction
- Cognition & Learning
- Social-Emotional Strengthening
- Executive Functioning

You will take the NAILEP at three distinct points throughout this program - at the beginning, middle and end. You can chart your scores on the adjacent page.

Type the URL in your browser to access your NAILEP Teacher Strengths from Legacy Education Group:
https://www.legacy-ed.com/nailep-access-members-unique-password-individual43538924kjo78tgsfj3jh
Password: UniversalBestPractices

YOUR NAILEP STRENGTHS PROFILE

COMMUNICATION & INTERACTION

INITIAL: _____

MIDDLE: _____

END: _____

LEARNING & COGNITION

INITIAL: _____

MIDDLE: _____

END: _____

NEURODIVERSITY & INCLUSION
Learning Environments Profile

SOCIAL-EMOTIONAL STRENGTHENING

INITIAL: _____

MIDDLE: _____

END: _____

EXECUTIVE FUNCTIONING

INITIAL: _____

MIDDLE: _____

END: _____

Based on your initial NAILEP Strengths, list a few actions below you can take to strengthen your learning environment for all:

Immediate _____

Mid-term _____

Long-term _____

A SERIES OF INVITATIONS

Kind of funny, but not really...

Dear Newly Hired Schoolteacher,
Thank you for signing a contract to work here at Goodluck School. We promise that we will support you and students will behave perfectly. We will provide completely relevant professional development, have your back at all times, and pay you as you ought to be paid.

Fictionally Yours,
The School System

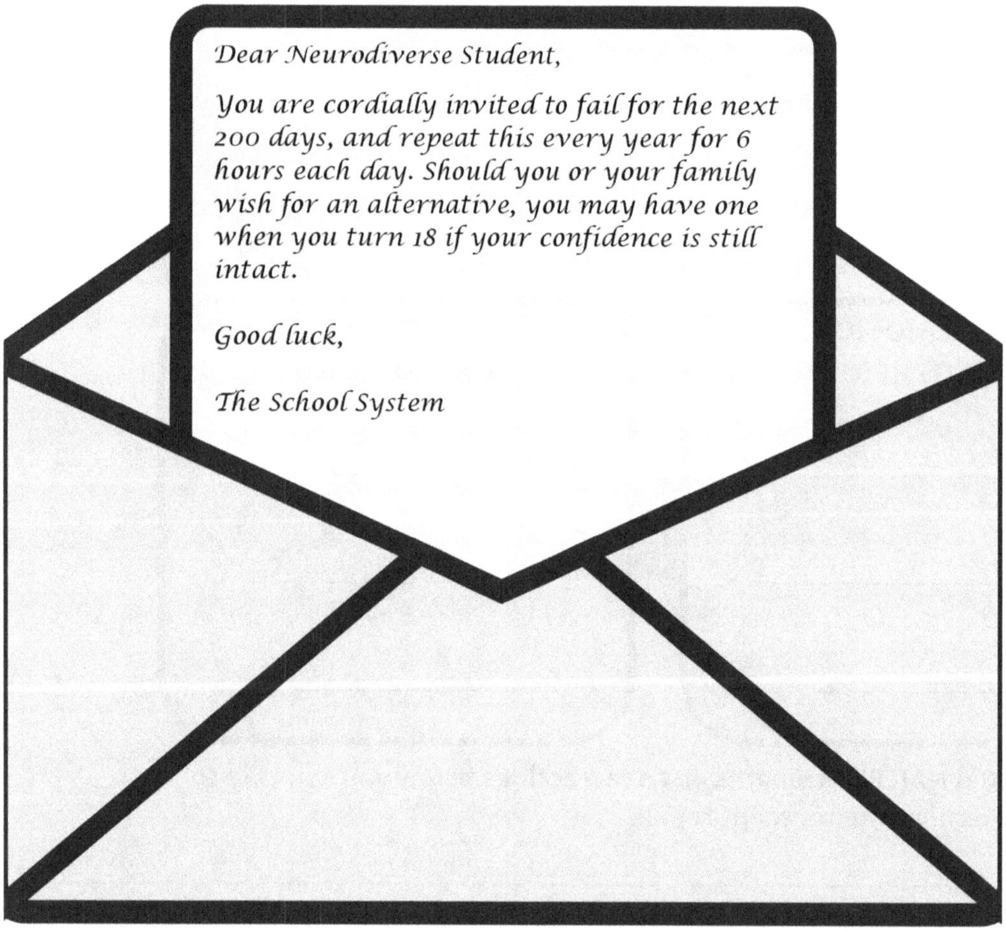

Dear Neurodiverse Student,

You are cordially invited to fail for the next 200 days, and repeat this every year for 6 hours each day. Should you or your family wish for an alternative, you may have one when you turn 18 if your confidence is still intact.

Good luck,

The School System

Let's change this.

Life is a series of competing invitations. Unless we possess a powerful and purposeful vision for the future, we choose whichever choice looks more appealing in the moment

Let's create a new invitation...

Dear Newly Hired Schoolteacher,

You are hereby invited to change the trajectory of neurodiverse students and their families for generations to come. Together we will leave a legacy of educational excellence.

Thank you for joining us.

What is the *current* spoken and unspoken "invitation" your students receive when they enter your learning environment?

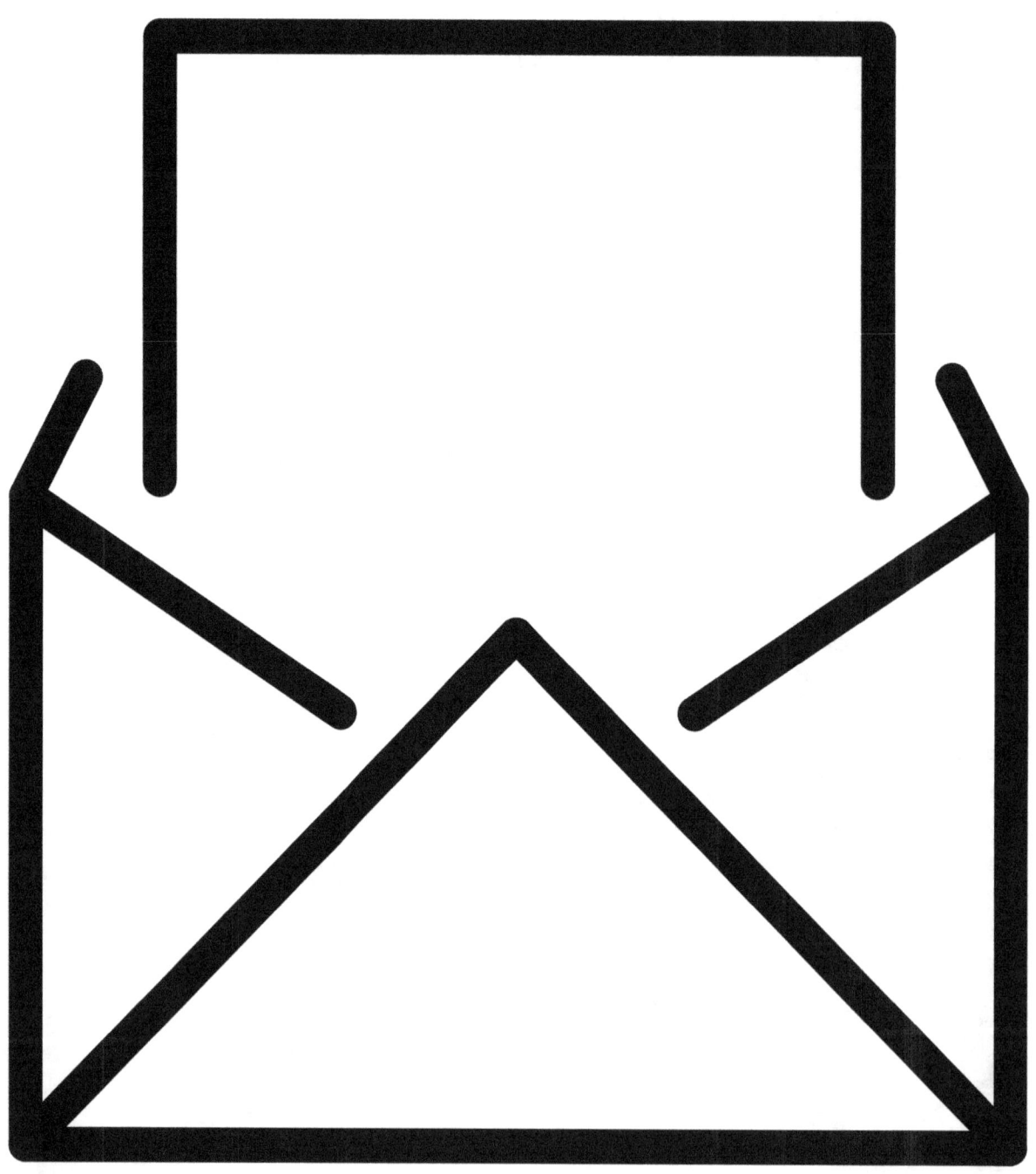

What *new* invitation do you aspire to offer all students (and families) who experience your learning environment?

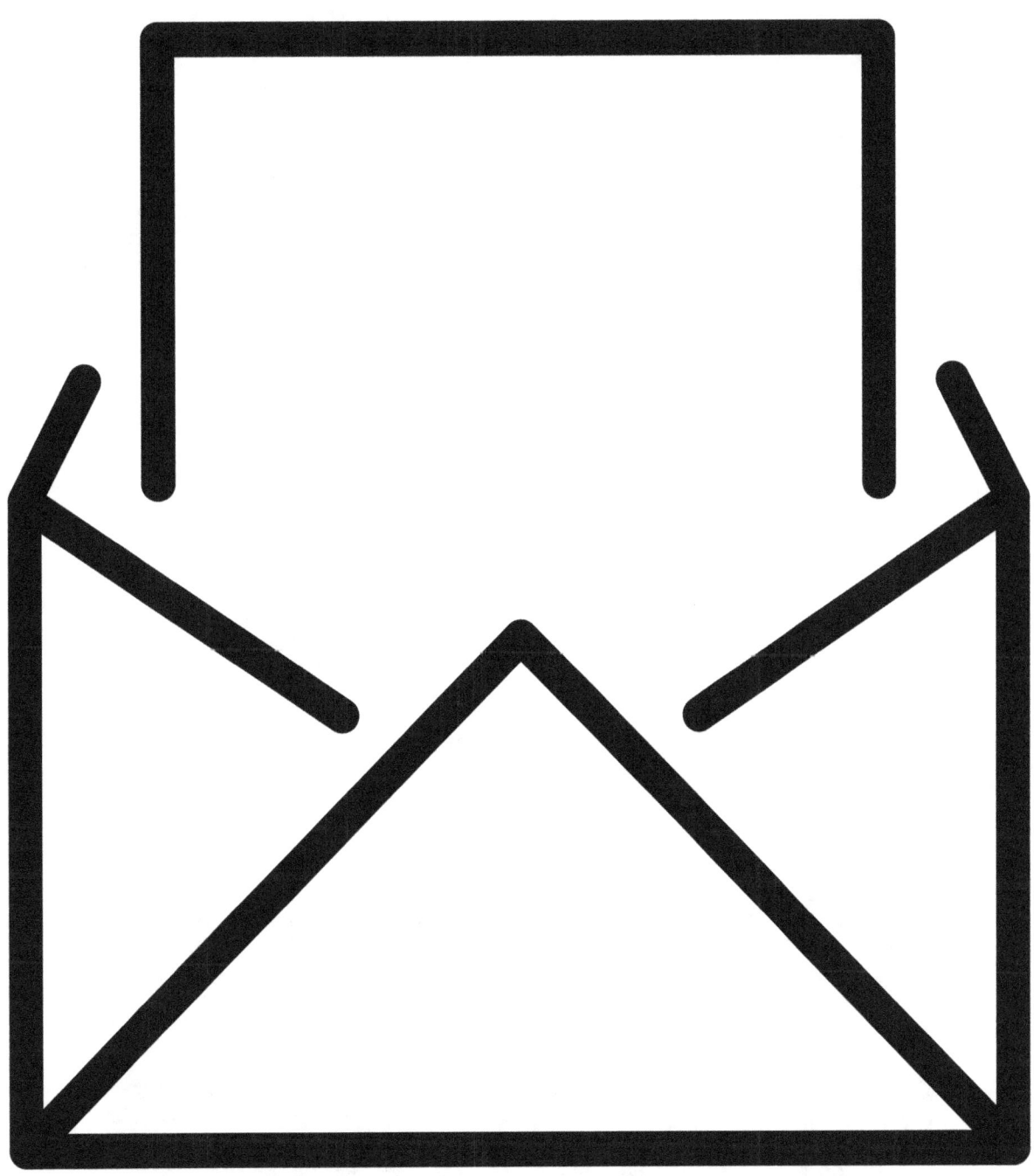

Part 1: Foundations for High Quality Learning Environments

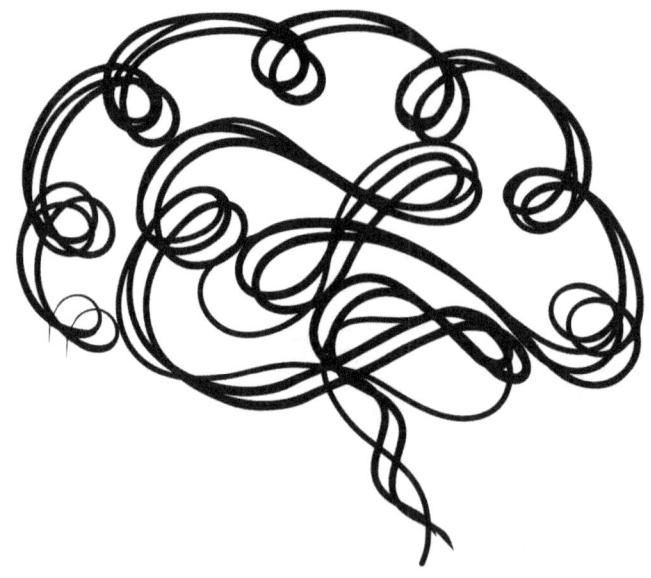

> The most difficult thing is the decision to act, the rest is merely tenacity.
> —Amelia Earhart

NEURODIVERSITY

WHAT IS IT?

Neurodiversity, defined as *individual brain differences that make everyone unique*, forms the cornerstone of our approach. We recognize that these differences manifest in the way individuals receive information, think, act, process, and express themselves. Rather than viewing these as deficits, our program embraces a "differences approach," where diverse representations are celebrated as valuable contributions to the learning environment.

Neurodiverse & Inclusive Learning Environments draw on the common pedagogical features of successful instruction. By understanding and addressing the Four Key strengths identified in Legacy Education Group's Neurodiversity & Inclusive Learning Environments Profile (NAILEP©), educators gain insights into creating learning environments that draw out the strengths of their students, including those with strengths and differences in:

1. Communication & Interaction
2. Learning & Cognition
3. Social Emotional Strengthening
4. Executive Functioning

LEGACY EDUCATION
Learning Together

NEURODIVERSITY
GENERAL STRENGTHS

Convenience has caused many to adopt what we call a "deficits model" for approaching neurodiversity in schools. Although we take these into account, the model and pathways proposed in this book will focus on the strengths and abilities of learners. The figure below highlights the adopted approach and philosophy.

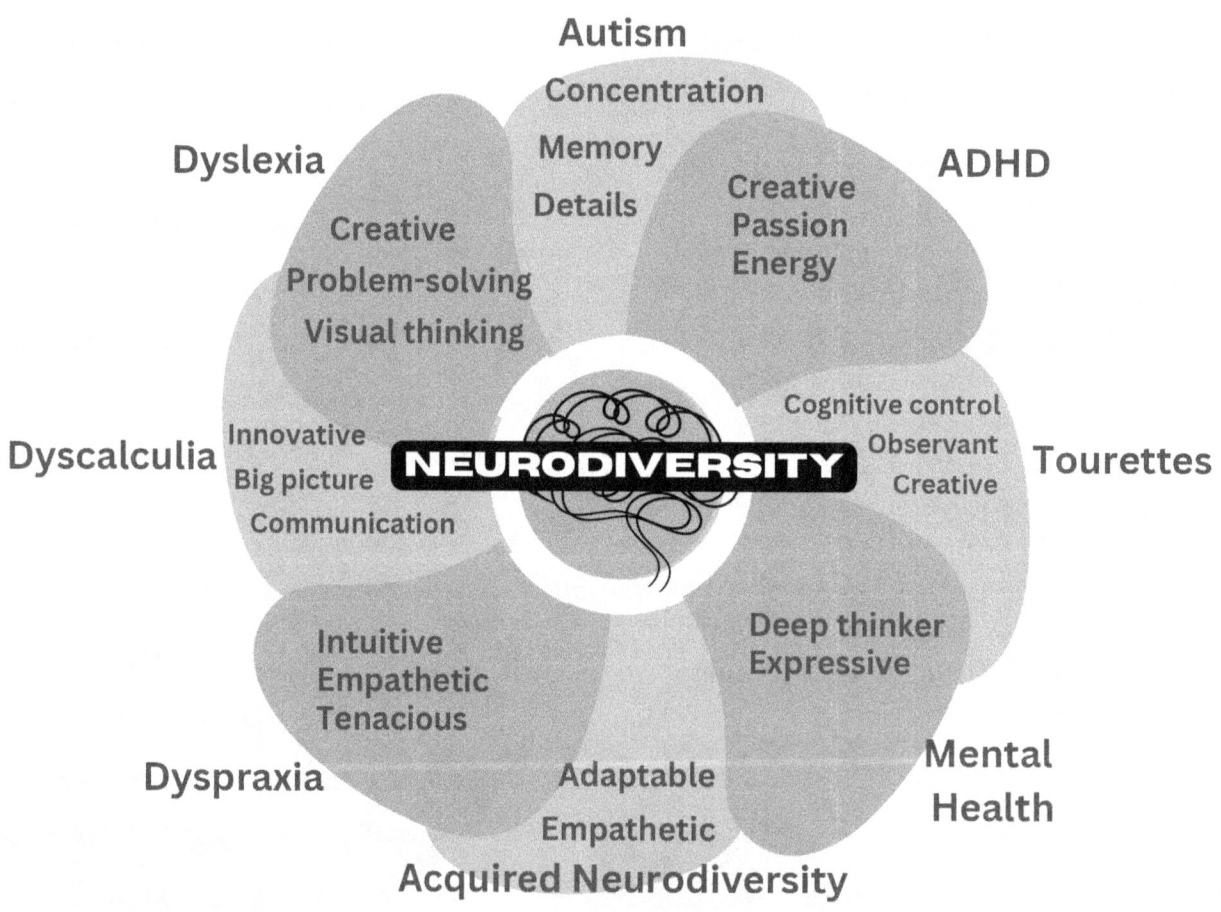

WHY NOW?

Addressing all of the challenges that arise in a classroom can feel like playing "whack-a-mole" at the arcade. However, *educationalists* who know how to use their strengths to create Neurodiverse & Inclusive Learning Environments do not react to challenges in this way. They instead create opportunities for students in their classroom to thrive before they even set foot in the school. Think of this book as the "set up"; that is, the actions you take prior to students setting foot in your learning space or classroom.

OUR MISSION

If there is one line you take away from this Program - although we hope there are many - it is this:

You cannot control students.
You can only control the environment you create for them.

PROGRAM
PRINCIPLES

This program advocates for effective instructional and pedagogical methods that have a positive impact on learning. As we develop our understanding of Legacy Education's Four Key Strengths (or *environmental considerations*) in designing learning environments, they can create spaces that offer opportunities for all students to succeed and demonstrate knowledge. The **Simple View of Learning Environments** (see below) illustrates how the learning climate can influence students - positively and negatively. Effective learning environments support and develop *communication and interaction, learning and cognition, social-emotional strengths,* and *executive functioning*. You will naturally be gifted in one or more of these areas, and this program will help you understand how to further leverage and develop your natural teaching abilities to reach your full potential.

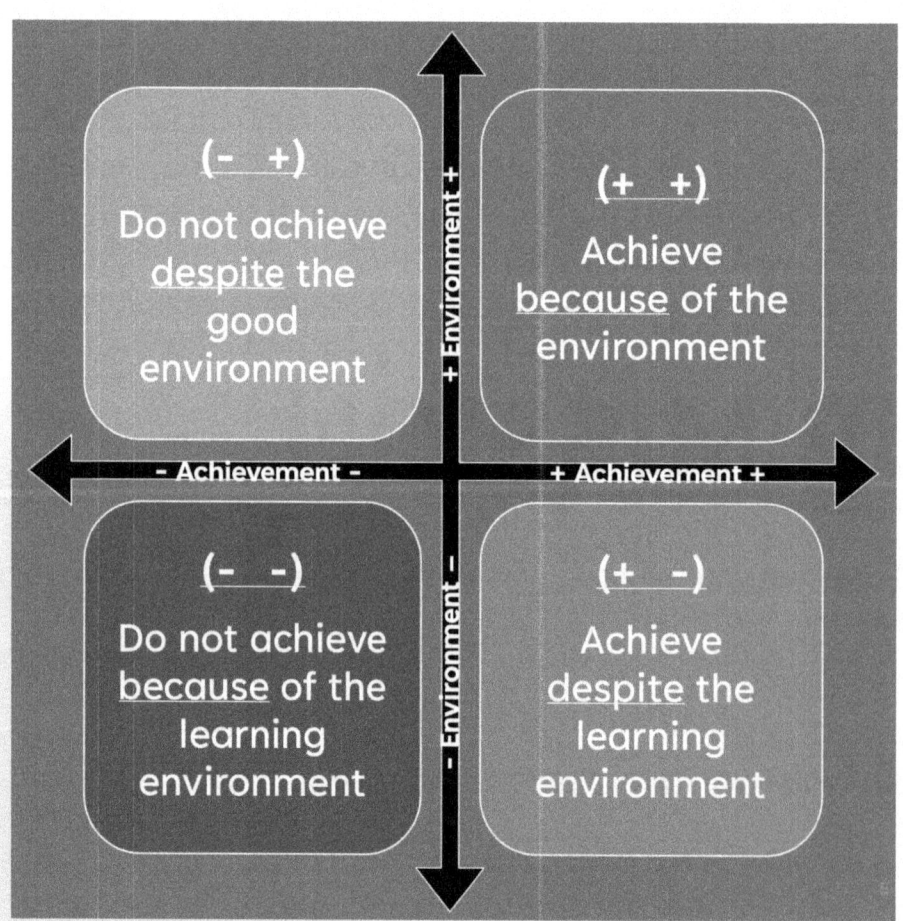

Learning Environments & MTSS

Schools around the world are embracing multi-tiered systems of support (MTSS) to improve their systems for both preventative and responsive support and instruction for at-risk learners' academic and behavioral skills. Our Program is rooted in the foundational best practices for *all* learners, including those with learning differences, and is compatible with all levels of effective MTSS. In fact, Neurodiverse & Inclusive Learning Environments form the foundation for MTSS to succeed, which is why we call this program "Universal Best Practices for All Learners".

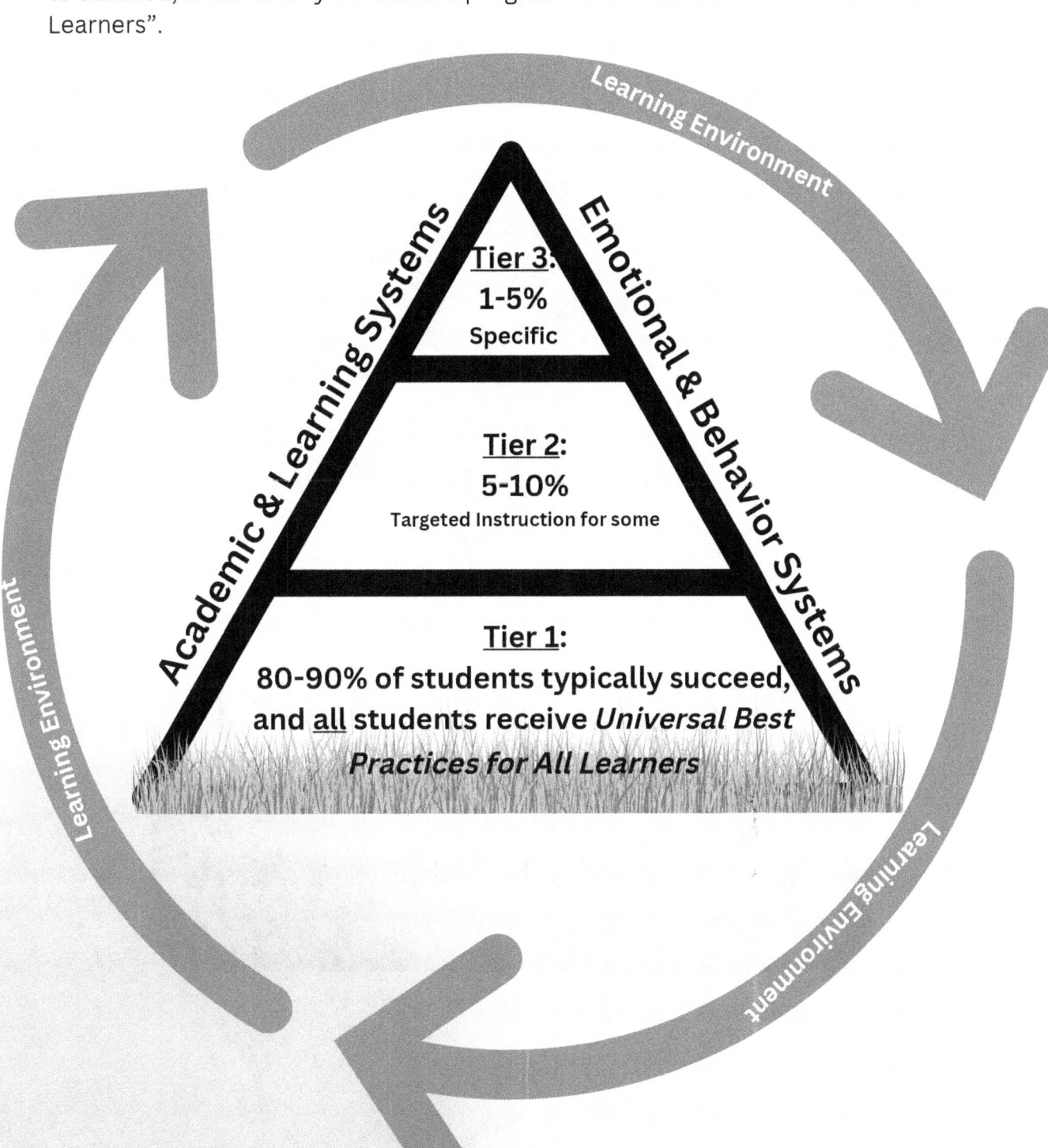

> The best time to plant a tree was 20 years ago.
> The second best time is now.
> —Chinese Proverb

ABOUT
LEGACY EDUCATION

Legacy Education specializes in universal education development services to champion schools, families, and educational organizations. With a distinctive focus on neurodiversity through a strengths-based lens, our tailored services ensure your aspirations are at the forefront of all we do.

"Learning together to leave a legacy of educational excellence"

PRACTICAL

Our programs are low-burden and high-impact, allowing you to focus on what you do best. It takes consistency and a concerted effort to create learning environments for all, and it won't always be easy. We promise that by doing so, you will give all students the opportunity to succeed in school and beyond.

COLLABORATIVE

Healthy things grow.
The healthiest things grow together.
We believe the most meaningful learning takes place in community *and* relationships - both of which take time to develop. Our programs and professional development keep collaboration at the heart of all we do.

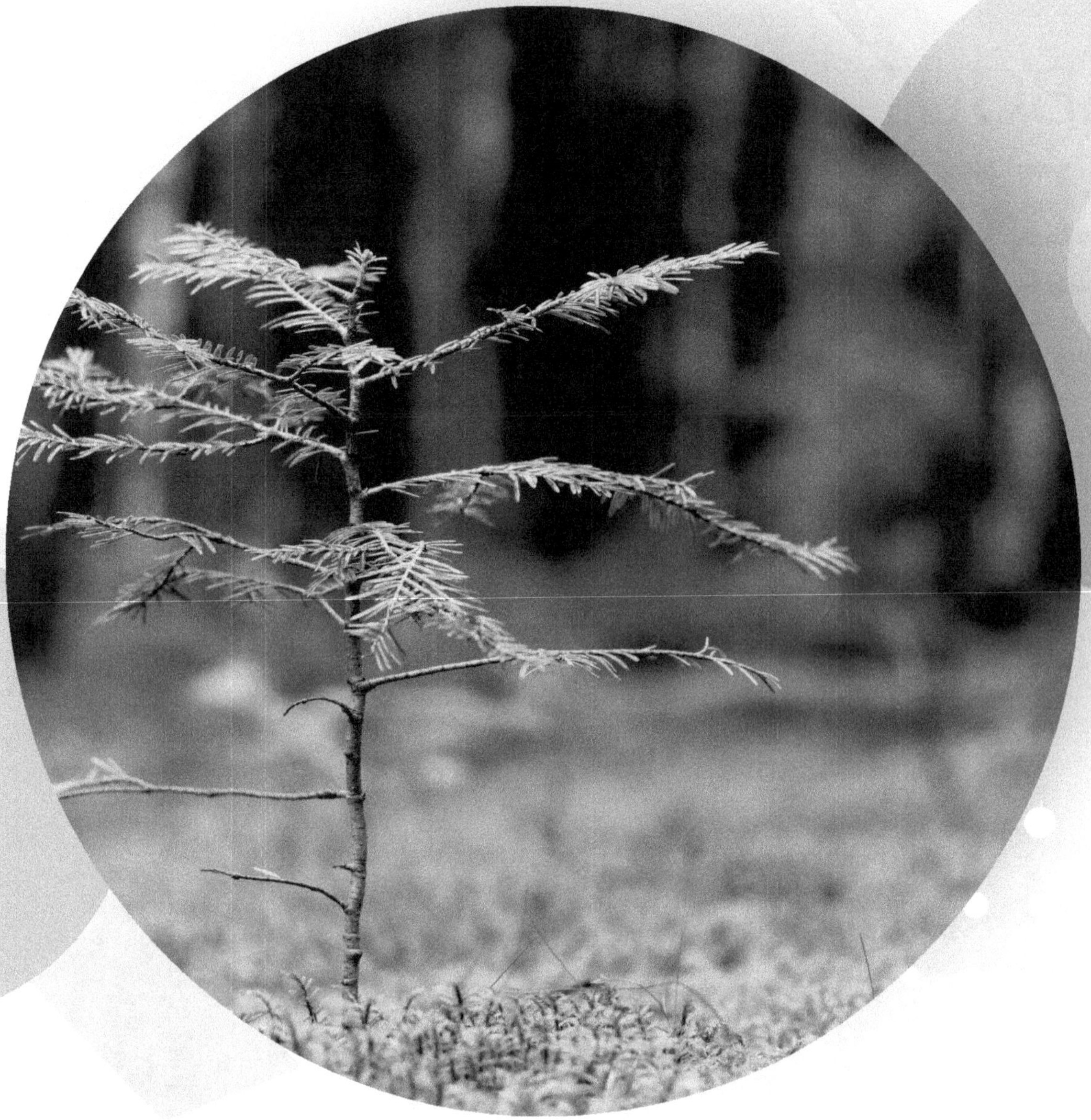

OUR JOURNEY
BEGINS HERE

Let's Grow Together

Performance or Growth Mindset?

| I believe that effort can lead to success | ← 100% agree | ← | ← | ← | ↑ | ↑ | ↑ | ↑ | 100% agree ↑ | I believe that ability leads to success |

| I am concerned to be seen as able and to perform well in others' eyes | ← 100% agree | ← | ← | ← | ↑ | ↑ | ↑ | ↑ | 100% agree ↑ | I believe in my ability to improve and learn, and not to be fixed or stuck |

| I prefer challenging tasks whose outcome reflects my approach | ← 100% agree | ← | ← | ← | ↑ | ↑ | ↑ | ↑ | 100% agree ↑ | I seek satisfaction from doing better than others |

| I emphasise competition, public evaluation | ← 100% agree | ← | ← | ← | ↑ | ↑ | ↑ | ↑ | 100% agree ↑ | I gain satisfaction from personally defined success at difficult tasks |

| I talk to myself: when engaged in a task I talk myself through it | ← 100% agree | ← | ← | ← | ↑ | ↑ | ↑ | ↑ | 100% agree ↑ | When the task is difficult, I display helplessness: "I can't do x" |

© Adam Meyersieck 2017

INTRODUCTION TO
THE FOUR KEY STRENGTHS

The *Neurodiverse & Inclusive Learning Environments Program* draws on long-held research-based features of successful instruction and pedagogy. By championing the Four Key Strengths, educators gain insights for creating learning environments that meet the diverse needs of their students.

We will dive deeper into each of these throughout this program, and will briefly define each in the next few pages before the Deep Dives.

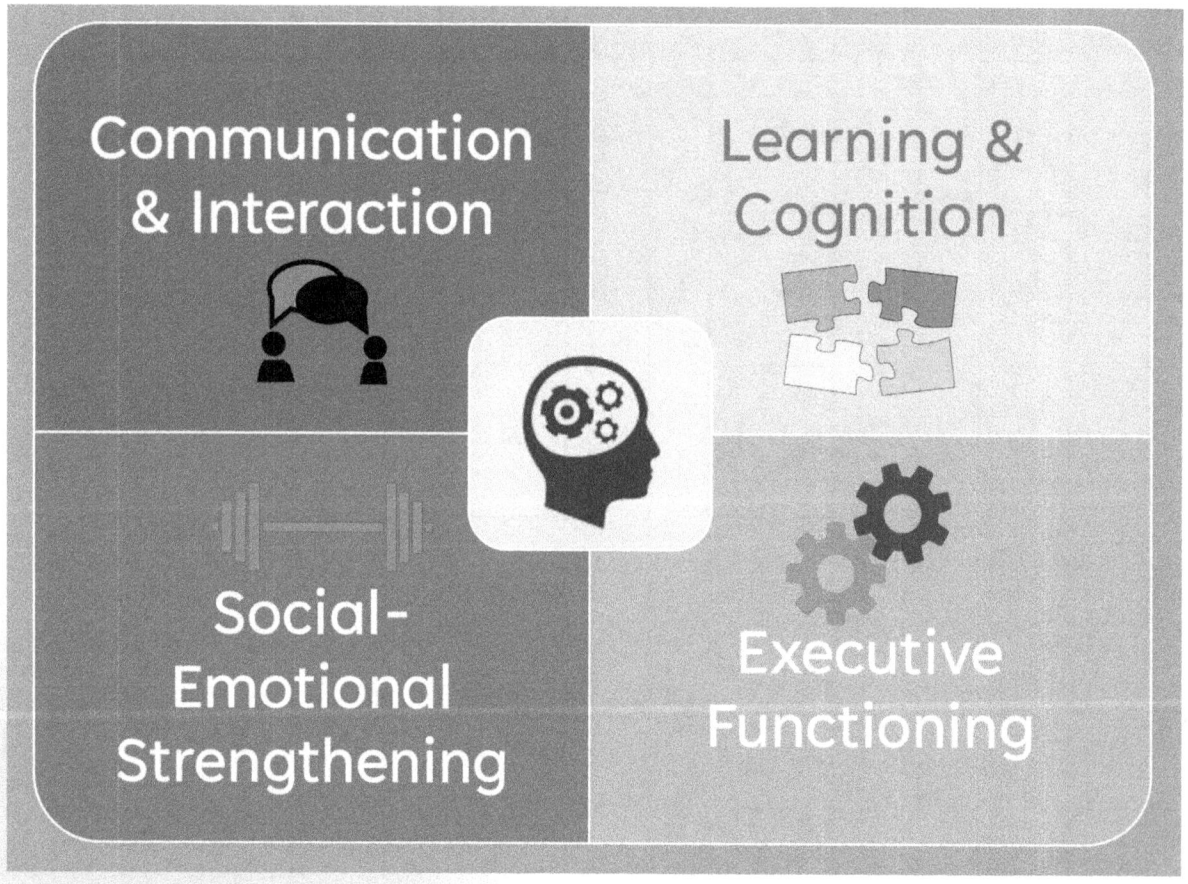

COMMUNICATION & INTERACTION (C&I)

One of the most basic needs of all humans is to successfully communicate and interact with others, however, many students find this more challenging than others. This specifically helps you identify, target, and remove systemic environmental barriers to this vital skill. This is done by addressing any environmental deficits and providing schools (and individual professionals) with a roadmap to ensure maximum success of neurodiverse learners.

A number of students have Communication & Interaction (C&I) differences to varying degrees. Some of them receive additional accommodations and support from other professionals, while others have less-obvious differences. As a C&I Champion, you anticipate this with the systems and strategies highlighted in this program.

Differences often associated with C&I can include:
- **Speech/Language**
- **Autism (and Autism Spectrum Condition)**
- **Other receptive and expressive communication differences**

LEARNING & COGNITION (L&C)

Everyone learns and processes information differently. It can be easy to assume students will understand grade-level content based on their age or the curriculum, but students with Learning & Cognition (L&C) differences may find certain aspects of instruction challenging.

To ensure all students can reach their full potential in your classroom, it is crucial to optimize the key strengths in this program. By establishing clear, systems and routines at the beginning of the year, you can eliminate systemic barriers to learning and help students with these differences to thrive.

Often, students who have been identified as having these neurodiversities receive special educational support via an individualized education plan (IEP) or 504 Plan (USA)

In the following pages, you will find specific action points to help students with Learning & Cognition differences reach their potential. By implementing these strategies, you can create an environment that is supportive and inclusive for these learners.

L&C differences may include:
- **Dyslexia (specific learning differences in reading and/or writing)**
- **Dyscalculia (specific learning differences in mathematics)**
- **Attention Deficit Hyperactivity (ADHD)**
- **Autism**
- **Processing difficulties**

SOCIAL-EMOTIONAL STRENGTHENING

Social-Emotional Strengthening (SES) is an essential aspect of helping neurodiverse learners develop resiliency, character, independence, and cooperative social skills. A school-wide approach that utilizes the tenets of SES, including character and integrity development, can lead to improved academic outcomes that include better attitude toward self, community engagement, and improved academic performance.

Tenets of successful SES can include learning that promotes:

- **Character education**
- **Learning resiliency**
- **Establishing healthy boundaries for self and others**
- **Self-awareness**
- **Self-management**
- **Responsible decision-making**
- **Relationship skills**
- **Social awareness**

EXECUTIVE FUNCTIONING (EF)

Executive function (EF) and self-regulation skills are the mental processes that enable us to plan, focus attention, remember instructions, and juggle multiple tasks successfully. The three main utilities of EF include:

Cognitive Flexibility- Cognitive flexibility is the ability to view a variety of situations through different perspectives. Individuals with cognitive flexibility are able to find success despite unexpected issues that arise. These students learn how to adjust to change, adapt their thinking about issues when new facts present themselves, and can improvise well when sudden changes take place.

Working Memory- Working memory is the ability to hold information in mind and to creatively reorganize it to create new information. This is not to be confused with short-term memory, which is the ability to follow through with an instruction or information in sequential order. While working memory can rely on short-term memory, it also permits individuals to:

- relate different ideas to one another
- reflect on past ideas and connect it to future implementation
- remember questions as you give attention to ongoing dialogue
- make sense of new information and relate it to current events

Inhibition Control (including self-control)- Inhibitory control is one's ability to control responses or actions and limit impulsivity. Many young people, including those with attention differences, find it difficult to control or hold back behavior even if they know it is unconstructive.

An unexamined life is not worth living.
—Socrates

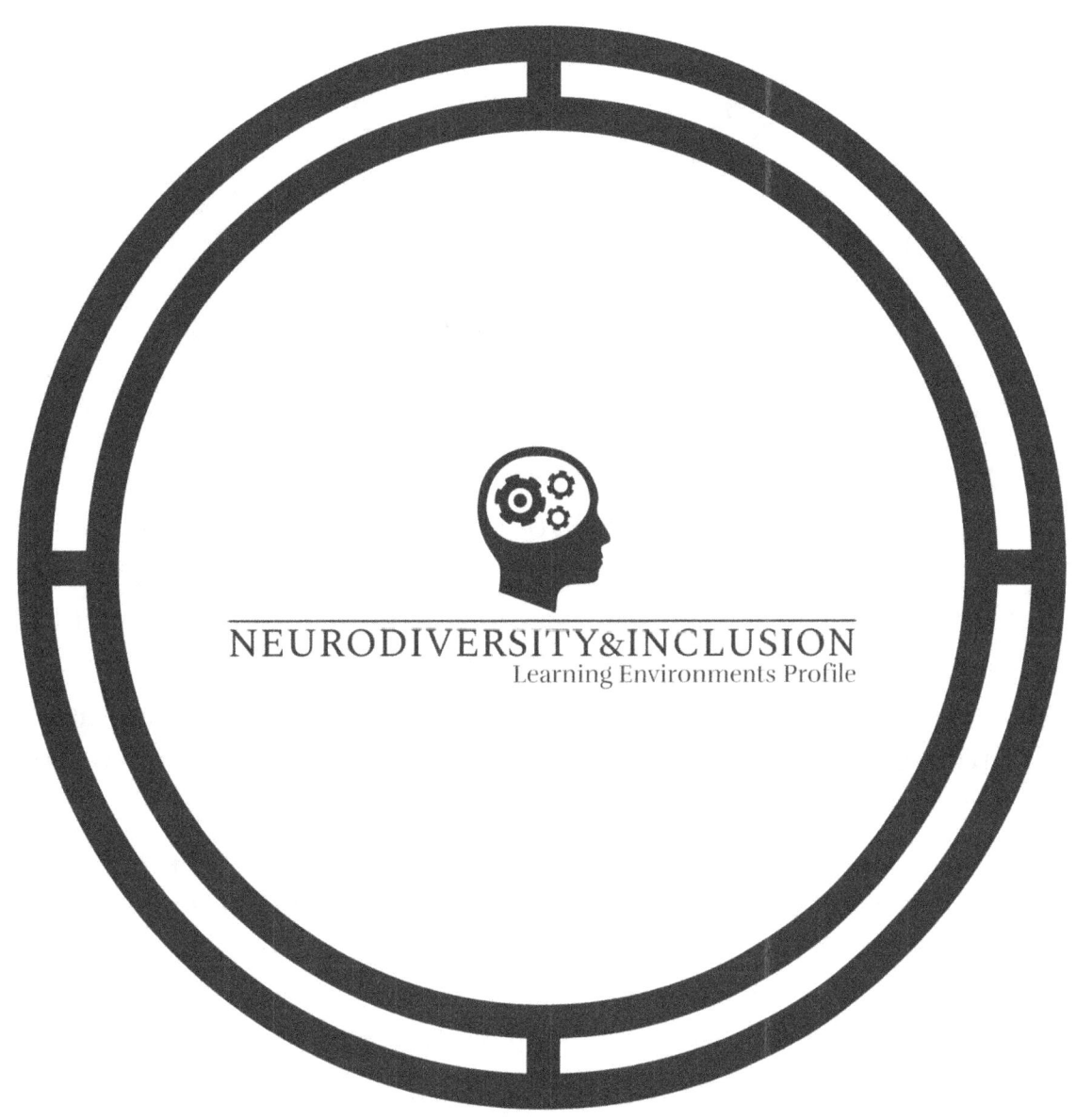

The Neurodiversity & Inclusion Learning Environments Program
(NAILEP)

The NAILEP is a school-wide and classroom environmental measure that helps you better understand your strengths as a teacher. We believe ambitious educationalists who create Neurodiverse & Inclusive Learning Environments are unapologetic in their pursuit of optimized learning spaces where all students can learn together. Legacy Education works with schools and organizations to increase their professional capacity to address the Four Key Strengths outlined here. After taking the NAILEP (see page 5), you will have the opportunity to strengthen your learning environment and pedagogy throughout this book or through additional training from Legacy Education. Visit www.Legacy-Ed.com to learn how we can help.

This book supports teacher pedagogical strengths in four key areas of neurodiversity. We call these the Four Key Strengths. Your results will highlight the areas in which you naturally tend to excel at, and those that might require your attention. Your accompanying results will help you solidify your strengths and point you in the right direction for areas you may want to develop. This manual is best used alongside your individual NAILEP Teacher Strengths results, but is written in such a way that it can be used on its own.

If you decide to take the NAILEP, you will receive an action guide based on your specific results that will encourage you in multiple ways, including:

- **Reflect on your overall score** in each of the Four Key Strengths. What do you think it says about your learning environment and your approach? Do you believe it accurately captures how your learning environment takes into consideration the needs of your neurodiverse learners?
- **Take some time** and look through the Action Guide to determine whether it is a true reflection of the learning environment you have created. Don't just jump to the radar chart and make assumptions. Dig deeper into each area of strength and development, and ask yourself, "What single step can I take tomorrow to make this even better?" Then keep asking yourself that question.

- **Triangulate your results**. After you have reflected on your NAILEP scores, share your results with a trusted colleague, mentor, or leader. Ask them if they believe it is a true reflection of your learning environment, and discuss how you can work together to improve pedagogical practice.

Once you have taken the NAILEP, you now have an effective baseline measure from which you can continue to develop your learning environment and support others' pursuit of Neurodiverse & Inclusive Learning Environments.

To discover your unique NAILEP Teacher Strengths from Legacy Education Group, turn to page 5.

ACTIVITY

In the space below, take a few minutes to consider the following questions:
- Describe what your learning environment **looks** like.
- What does learning **sound** like?
- How do you best **communicate** with your students?
- What **tools/resources** do students have available to effectively interpret or communicate what they know about a subject or activity?

Use this activity as a baseline for the your journey through this book.

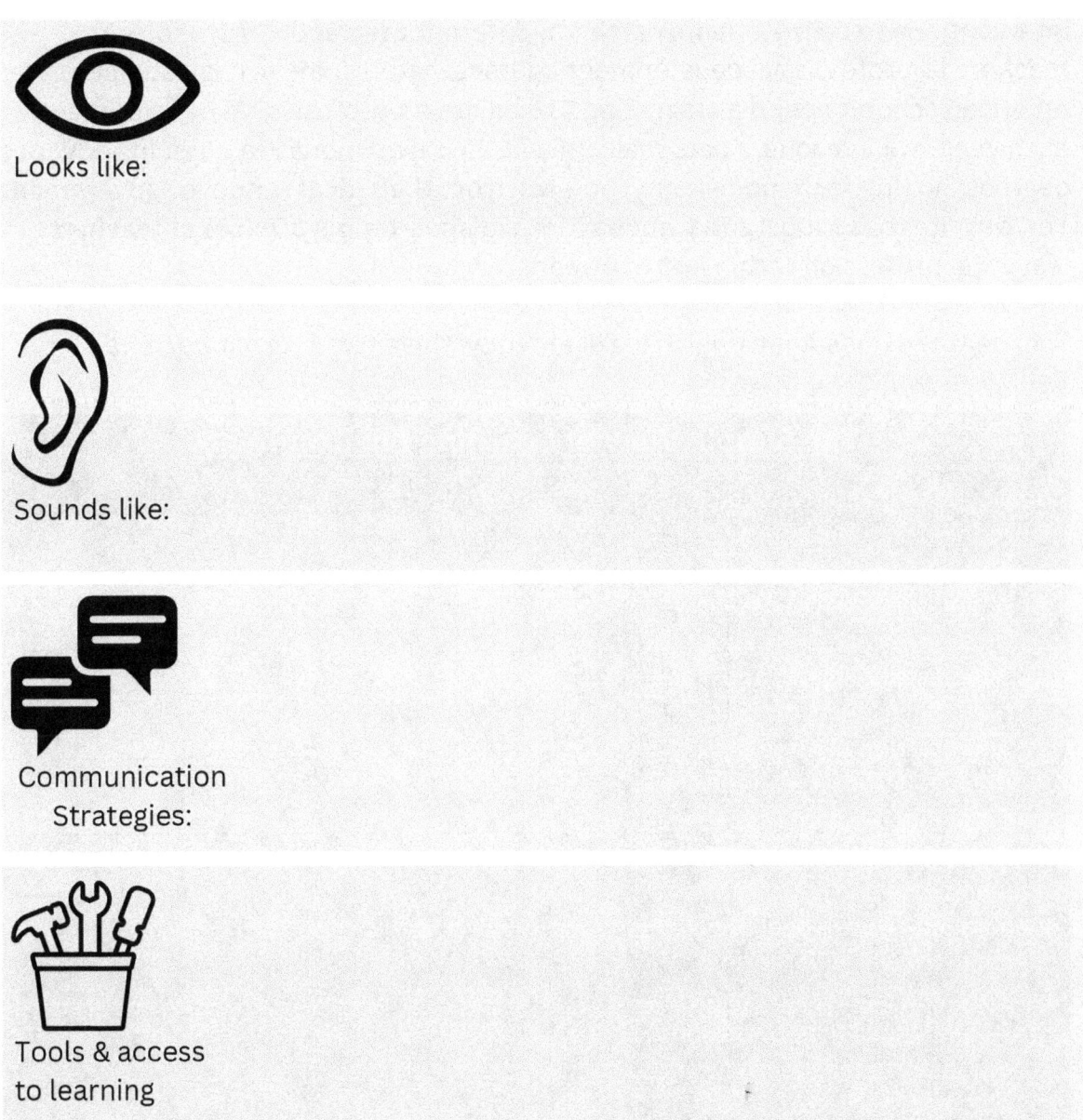

THE SIMPLE VIEW OF LEARNING ENVIRONMENTS

Traditionally, school and classroom learning environments favored students who possessed the ability to sit still, listen attentively (or at least quietly), and complete assignments. Those who succeeded were often students who understood the nuances of the educational system and skillfully maneuvered within it. However, the landscape has changed, and today's students arrive at school with a wide range of differences that the current education system was unprepared to address.

In response, schools have undertaken significant efforts to meet these diverse needs. They have invested in new curricula, implemented reading and math interventions to help students catch up, differentiated activities, and sent teachers to professional development courses. Astonishingly, it is estimated that American schools spend a staggering $18 billion on professional development each year, while teachers personally invest their own money in pursuing advanced degrees, hoping for a modest pay increase from their local school or government. Yet, despite these substantial endeavors, a disheartening 30-45% of teachers leave the profession within just five years.

This begs the question to which we likely know the answer: *Is our current approach truly effective?*

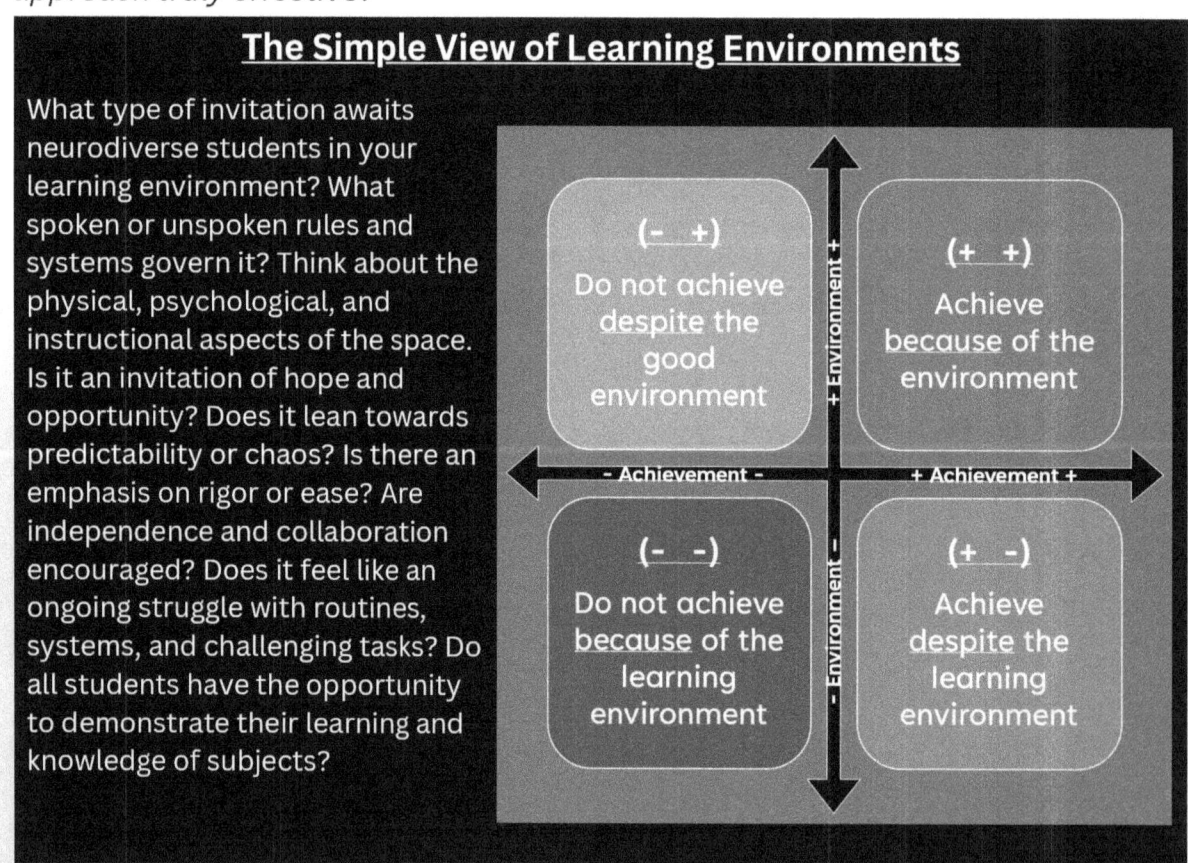

Each student will fit into one of these four quadrants. It might look different in each lesson (or even within a lesson), so take a moment to reflect on the students you support and how you support them. In the Deep Dive we will consider the following for each of the Four Key Strengths:
- *Classroom routines*
- *Lesson/activity structures*
- *How you communicate, verbally and nonverbally*
- *Different methods students have to demonstrate knowledge*
- *Tools students have available to succeed*
- *Collaborative opportunities given to students*
- *How students cooperate together to improve knowledge*
- *The systems or methods you use for teaching and learning- do they help or hinder?*

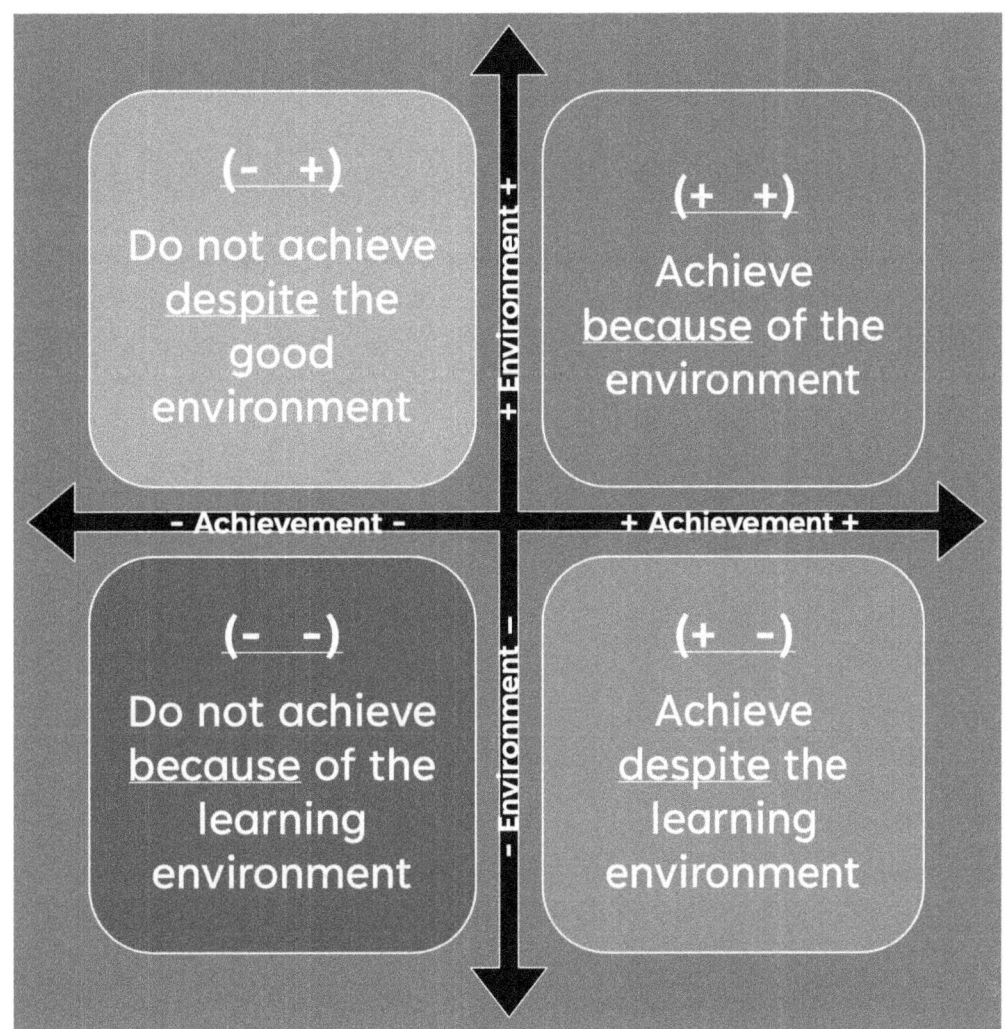

ACTIVITY

Fill in the *Simple View of Learning Environments* chart below. Consider a number of the students you teach. Where might they "fit"? For now, just write their initials in the quadrant you think currently best describes their achievement.

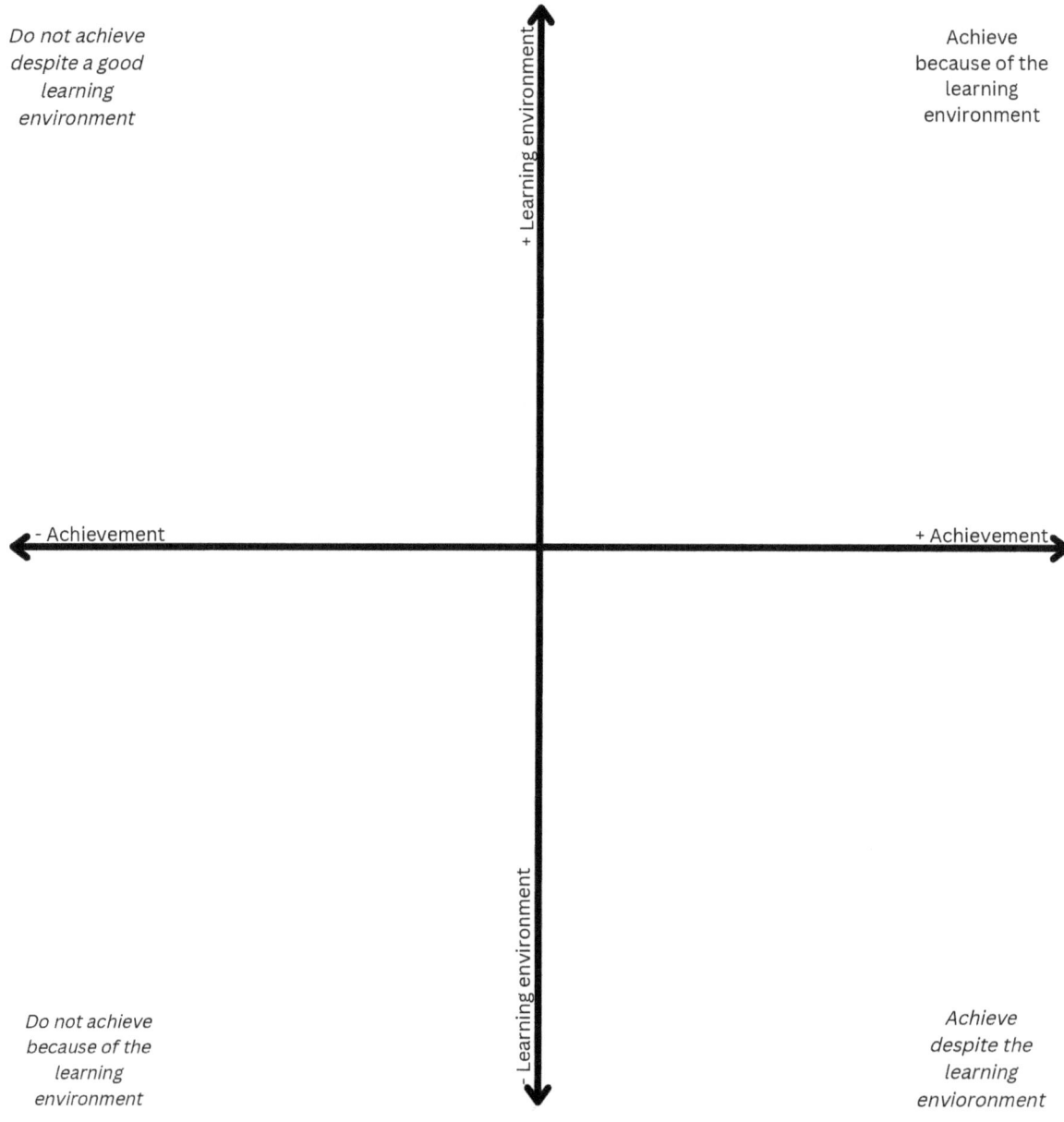

Achieve because of a good learning environment + +

Traditionally, students who excelled in school attributed their success to the conducive learning environment that favored those who could sit still, listen attentively, complete assignments accurately, and so forth. In essence, these students understood the dynamics of the educational system and knew how to navigate it effectively. However, in recent years, numerous schools have made concerted efforts to revamp their curriculum, implement interventions, and offer differentiated lessons to meet growing student need. The students who continued to thrive were those who adeptly adapted to the evolving educational landscape. Do your neurodiverse students achieve because of your learning environment?

THINK ABOUT IT

Take a moment to reconsider the students described in this quadrant. Would they excel in *any* educational system? How proficient are their communication and interaction skills? What about their cognition and learning abilities? Do they possess strong socio-emotional skills and executive functioning capabilities?

Chances are, these students face few in these domains, or concerted efforts have been made to help them overcome them. They likely possess the necessary skills to thrive in any school system worldwide.

Achieve despite a poor learning environment + -

FEATURES OF POOR LEARNING ENVIRONMENTS

We all know it when we see it, but some common features of poor learning environments might include:

- Bad lighting
- Noise (echoes, bad flooring, repetitious commands from staff etc.)
- Temperature
- Disorganized planning and activities
- Lack of boundaries
- Inconsistent consequences
- Ineffective layout
- Overcrowding
- Arguing between children, and between children and adults
- Over-reliance on single-methods of teaching and learning
- Unsafe learning space(s)

Many staff in schools find themselves recovering from decades of mismanagement, high teacher turnover, and other unfortunate circumstances. Despite a poor learning environment (and against all odds), a few fortunate students are miraculously able to find lifelong success. They may have impeccable willpower or determination, natural applied abilities, or they may come from a family that supports them in doing so.

THINK ABOUT IT

How would you describe or define a poor learning environment? Awareness of these features will help you avoid this pitfall.

Do not achieve because of the poor learning environment - -

Poor learning environments can have a significant negative impact on student achievement, well-being, and life trajectory. Students in such environments may face limited access to quality resources, inadequate instructional support, and lack of positive learning experiences. The absence of a learning environment that values neurodiversity and inclusion typically leads to student disengagement, low motivation, and reduced academic performance. Students may struggle to acquire essential knowledge and skills, resulting in lower levels of achievement and limited opportunities for future success. Additionally, the negative effects of a bad learning environment can extend beyond academics, affecting students confidence and overall well-being. Creating supportive and enriching learning environments is crucial to unlocking their full potential and promoting achievement both in and outside the classroom.

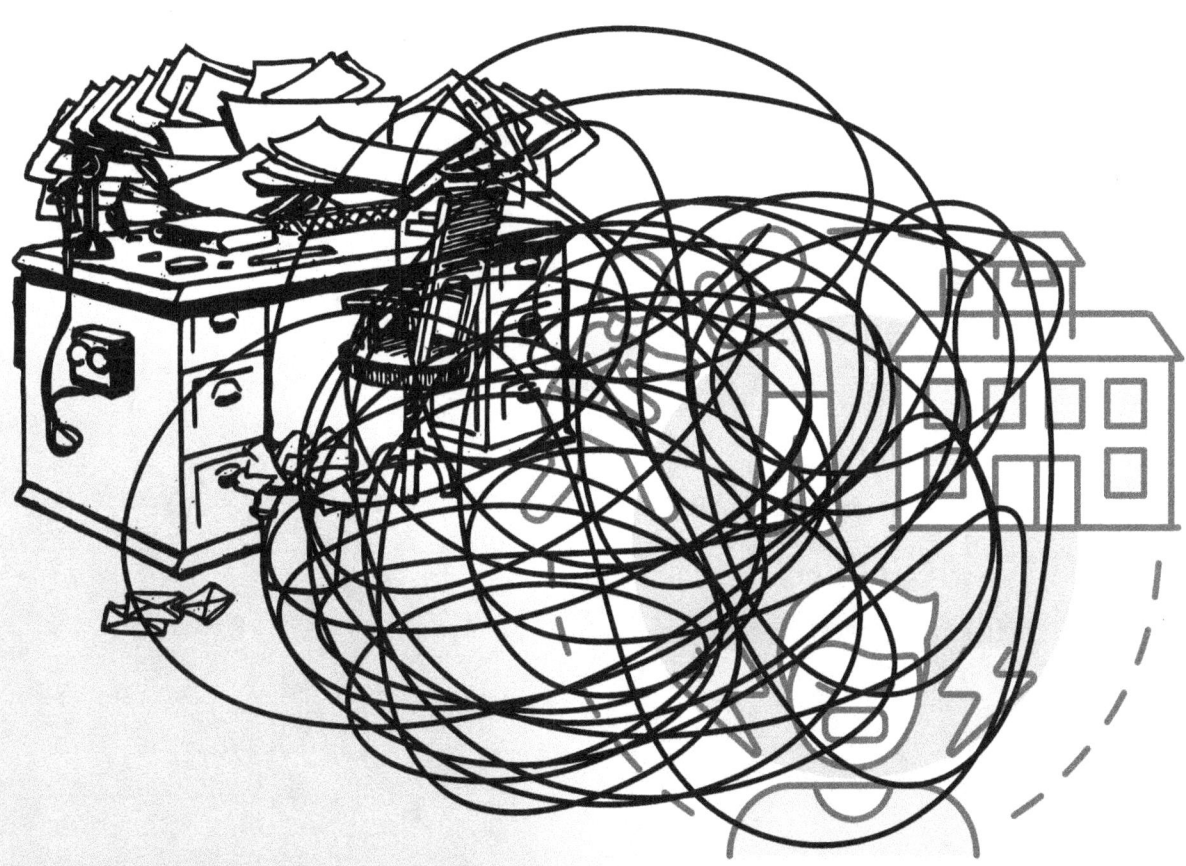

Do not achieve even in a good learning environment - +

Sometimes - despite experiencing a high-quality, neurodiverse, and inclusive learning environment - students still struggle to be successful in school. It can be difficult to understand why this might be the case, but it is vital that schools leave no stone unturned in their efforts to help students who fit into this quadrant. Continual reflection, evaluation of practices, open communication, personalized approaches, and ongoing professional development for educators are essential components of this endeavor. By actively seeking to understand and address the specific needs and barriers faced by these students, education institutions can ensure that every opportunity is provided. Creating an inclusive environment requires a commitment to individualized support and a willingness to adapt and improve upon existing approaches. By doing so, institutions can empower students in this quadrant to overcome obstacles and reach their full potential in an inclusive and supportive educational setting.

THINK & SHARE
What are some reasons you think a student might not achieve in school, despite experiencing a high quality, inclusive learning environment?

> Start where you are. Use what you have. Do what you can.
> —Arthur Ashe

Part 2
The Four Key Strengths

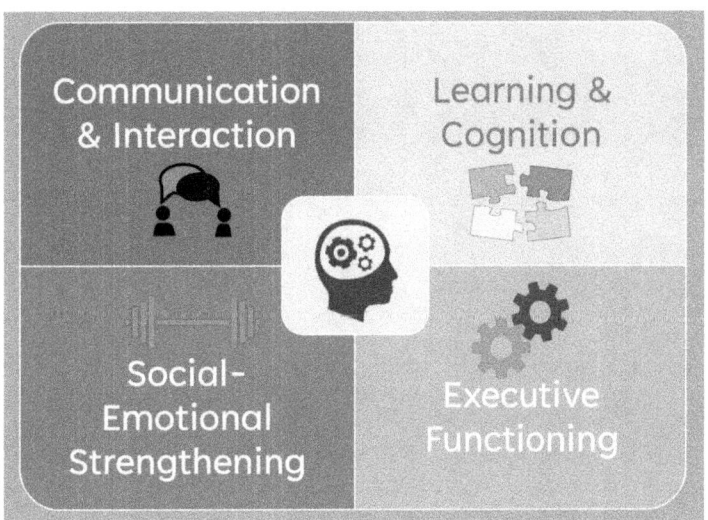

DEEP DIVE
COMMUNICATION & INTERACTION

Communication & Interaction (C&I) Warm-up

Reflect on what communication and interaction looks like and sounds like in your classroom. Note at least 5 observations for each question below.

Based on your NAILEP Teacher Strengths results, what would you say are your top 5 C&I Strengths?
1. _____
2. _____
3. _____
4. _____
5. _____

How do students with neurodiversities communicate and how do you support?
1. _____
2. _____
3. _____
4. _____
5. _____

Did any of your C&I results surprise you? If so, which one(s)?
1. _____
2. _____
3. _____
4. _____
5. _____

COMMUNICATION & INTERACTION PATHWAYS

The Communication & Interaction Pathway will take you on a transformative journey towards effective communication in a neurodiverse and inclusive classroom. In this section, you will encounter a series of NAILEP Strengths statements that serve as guiding principles for creating an environment that celebrates neurodiversity and fosters the growth of every student, regardless of their differences. By embracing these strengths and principles, and applying them diligently to your teaching practice, you will establish a learning environment that acknowledges and respects the diverse learning needs of all students. Through this approach, you will empower your students to flourish and unlock their full potential.

C&I 1
The class culture (e.g., rules, expectations, systems, etc.) is displayed, taught, modeled, and regularly reinforced through staff language.

There are multiple paths you can take to develop effective expectations in your classroom. Here are three of the most effective. The best rules and classroom culture expectations are simple:

Nearly every positive action you want students to take falls under these three categories. You can create a list under each of these with your students, but you may want to guide the conversation toward your intended outcome. Doing this will give students a sense of empowerment and ownership over the school and class community.

But if you're not convinced...
If these three are too vague for your students, be specific about your expectations, but keep these to fewer than six simple statements of community expectation. For example:
- We take care of school and individual property
- We always look, listen, and sit still when others are speaking
- We always try our best
- We always listen to teaching staff
- We speak and act kindly
- We celebrate individual and community success

What are the "rules" in your learning environment? Consider both the school and your classroom. On a scale of 0 to 5, how effective is each? *0 = not at all, 5 = followed all the time*

How do students demonstrate their understanding (or lack of understanding) of these?

How are rules supported by school leadership?

Make an list for what each of these should look like in your learning environment:

Respect

Responsibility

Safety

You will also need to be explicit about your classroom boundaries (i.e., those actions that violate trust and result in disciplinary action), so make these explicit and keep these to two or three:

- We never intentionally cause another person physical or mental harm
- We never destroy property intentionally

Displays, direct teaching, modeling, and regular reinforcement are powerful tools to establish consistent, predictable routines that protect all students and enable them to thrive in your learning environment.

Whichever avenue you take for establishing expectations for your class culture, you will need to review them consistently over the first days, weeks, and months of the school year.

C&I 2

Students are aware of and follow teacher cues for listening (e.g., a consistent attention grabber)

If you've taught for any number of years or remember your schooling, you'll be familiar with teacher phrases such as, "Stop, look, listen!" or "1-2-3, eyes on me." Some teachers even use the Pavlovian chime or a bell. Although these might seem basic, when used strategically and reinforced regularly, they can have a positive effect on classroom consciousness toward learning and routines.

How do you gain the attention of your students?

Verbal	Nonverbal	Any new ideas

C&I 3
Key vocabulary and concepts are emphasized visually and consistently reinforced with verbal language

Anchor charts (visual posters with key terminologies and concepts) are a vital aspect of any learning environment. When used strategically and minimally, they can be powerful tools that anchor student learning of key vocabulary and concepts.

When paired intentionally with teacher language, and that language meaningfully connects with students, neurodiverse individuals can form cognitive connections with their learning.

Which concepts are you teaching or have you taught that can be paired with new visuals and verbal language?

C&I 4
Key vocabulary and concepts are emphasized and consistently reinforced through gestures

More than just a 90s party game, *gestures* support your verbal language and visual anchors to make learning more meaningful. When students learn and create gestures, and pair these actions with curriculum language, they have a better chance of deeply embedding new concepts into their schema. Schema is how our brain organizes and categorizes information about the world.

Reflect on a previous lesson you taught and how you use gestures and actions to help students better understand concepts. Draw images below to illustrate the gestures you used (it's OK to use stick figures!).

C&I 5

Key vocabulary and concepts are emphasized and consistently reinforced through written language

Gauging your students' schema is a highly effective form of scaffolding new concepts and ideas. Although reinforcing new concepts and vocabulary through written language might seem like a no-brainer, teachers cannot simply splash information on the board and expect students to "get it." Instead, write in a way that connects to your students. If part of a multisyllabic word is familiar to them, use the parts of a word students might already have in their schema to support their understanding of the new word or concept. For example, you can form cross-curricular connections across different subjects to help students access their schematic knowledge of key vocabulary and concepts.

The 'Frayer Model' is a tool to help students understand new academic terms or complex vocabulary. It was created by Dorothy Frayer and her colleagues at the University of Wisconsin. This simple and effective graphic organizer helps students organize their thoughts and grasp difficult concepts.

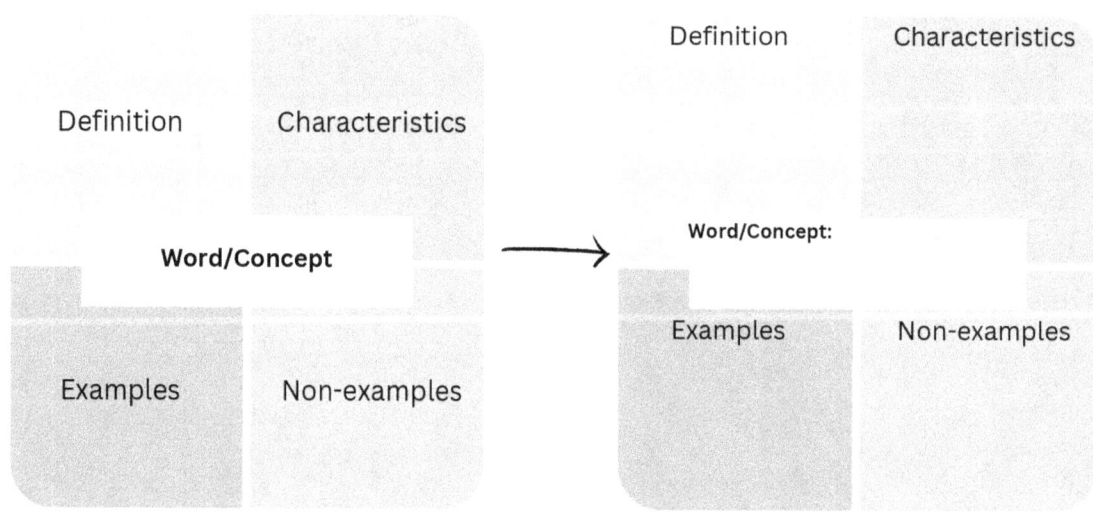

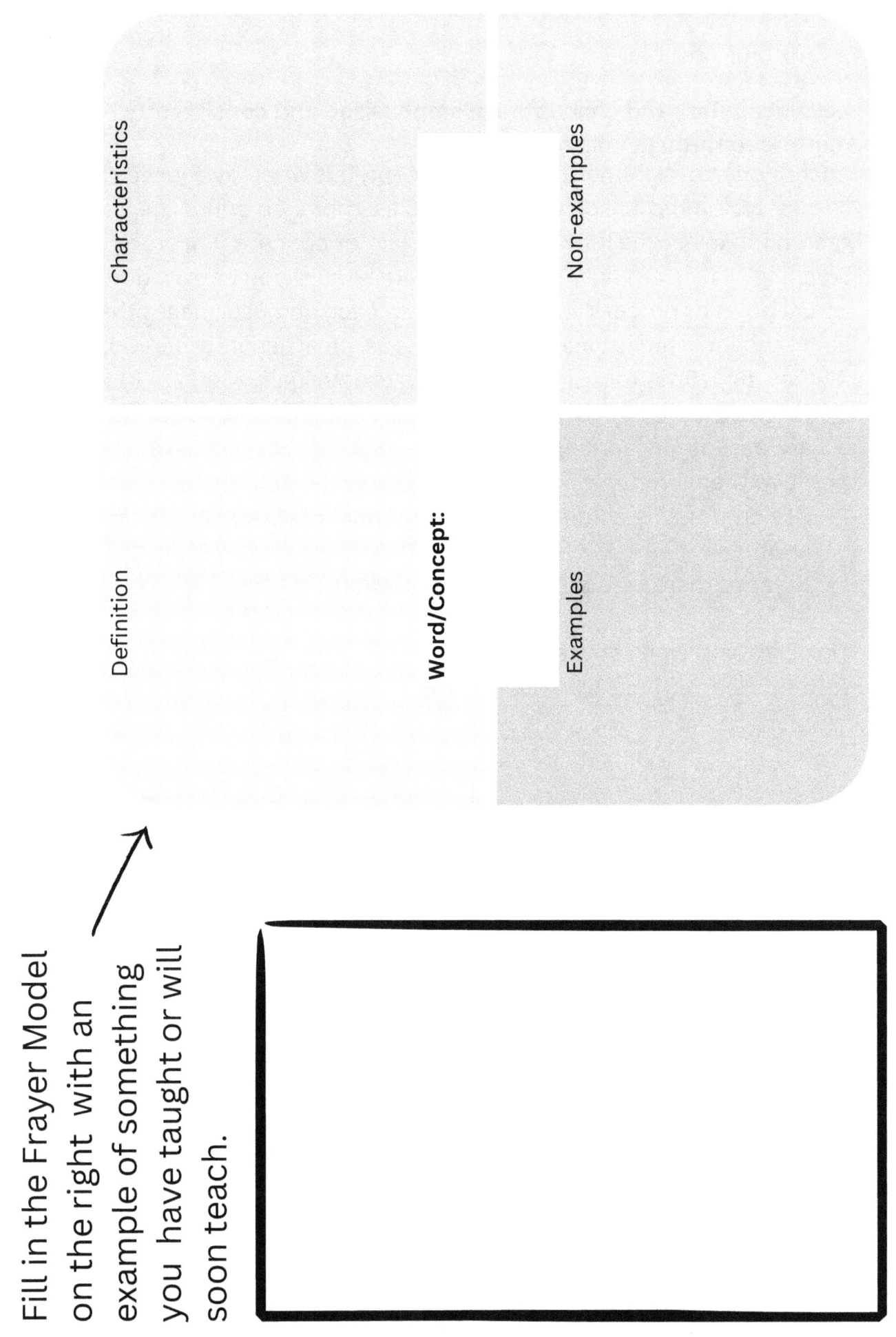

Fill in the Frayer Model on the right with an example of something you have taught or will soon teach.

Characteristics

Non-examples

Definition

Word/Concept:

Examples

C&I 6
Key vocabulary and concepts are emphasized and consistently reinforced through images

Anchor charts might not be a new concept, but when over-used they can get lost in the "display dross" in a classroom. An online image search for key terms for whichever subject or concept you are teaching will yield plenty of results, so make sure you narrow down the actual point or process you are trying to teach and use images that help "anchor" student learning to previously learned information. A few key guidelines for using anchor charts or visuals:

- Create them during your teaching with the students so students are part of the learning process
- Keep them brief
- Use contrasting colors that help key concepts stand out from one another
- Refer to them regularly during instruction

These visuals, when strategically used, go a long way for helping all students learn. Those who need it use it.

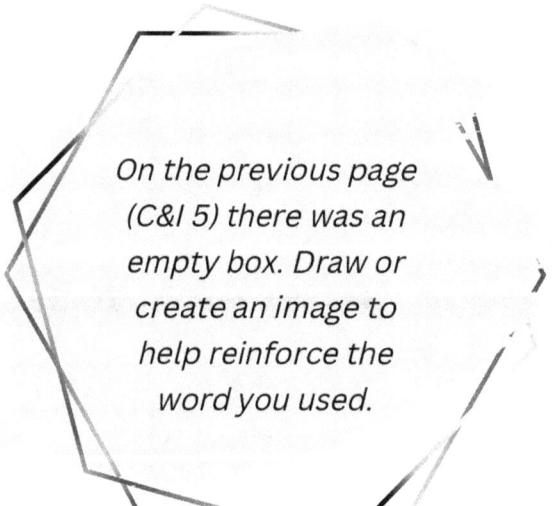

On the previous page (C&I 5) there was an empty box. Draw or create an image to help reinforce the word you used.

Reflection Notes: (a space for you to think on paper)

C&I 7
Multi-step instructions are broken down into smaller, sequential, manageable steps

We all know *the look*. You know, that "deer in the headlights" look, or that "I have no idea what I'm doing" look students give you after you told the class what to do. It is easy to tell your students to start writing (or to begin an activity). It is not as easy to break down the act of starting writing into smaller, manageable steps that some students need to know in order to prepare themselves for writing:

1. *Get a pencil*
2. *Get your notebook*
3. *Go back to your seat*
4. *Open it up to the first page*
5. *Check the assignment*
6. *Take 1-3 minutes to think about the instructions and what you will write*
7. *Begin writing*

Not every student will need this amount of specificity, but it is one way to avoid getting that "What the heck am I supposed to do?" look.

C&I 8
Students with C&I challenges are provided with written copies of the steps required to complete a task or assignment

Students with expressive and receptive language challenges have difficulties with expressing and receiving messages. Similar to a task analysis, checklists provide written and visual reminders to students about how to complete a task. It could be as basic as:

- Write your name and date on the paper
- Read the directions
- Pause and think "What am I being asked to do?"
- Begin working
- Re-read directions if unsure what to do
- Ask at least 2 neighbors before asking teacher
- Work until you the assignment is finished, or time is up
- Hand your work into the designated space

C&I 9
Lesson content is delivered at a pace that enables all students to understand what is being asked

There is an inherent problem with most school curriculum - they focus on breadth rather than depth of knowledge, making this specific neurodiverse classroom climate strategy difficult to navigate. When delivering content, slow down your rate of speech and choose words carefully. This cuts out any unnecessary language that cause barriers to learning.

C&I 10
After delivering instruction or asking a key question, students are given time to process the information before answering or moving on to the next concept or idea

As a teacher, it is easy to ask questions and have a few select students immediately raise their hands to answer them. The problem is that it's usually the same students answering. To mitigate this, try saying:

"I am going to ask a question. If you know the answer, I do not want you to raise your hand. Instead, take 15 seconds to think about the answer on your own. Then, I will as you to share your thinking with a person next to you. Here's my question…"

C&I 11
All students are given the opportunity to communicate their learning or knowledge through various methods (e.g., multimedia, oral report, written report, etc.)

This requires preparation, which leads to better instruction. When you know how you will assess student knowledge, your teaching funnels into that assessment. Video, audio, written, and oral reports are great ways to measure your students' knowledge, and they give some students a new outlet for their creativity. It is important for you to provide a clear framework or rubric for what you expect and which skills they need to demonstrate, thus establishing a truly neurodiverse classroom.

Reflection Notes:

C&I 12
The use of "impressive jargon" is minimized unless it is necessary to support, reinforce, or define concepts

Using big words can be fun and make students smile and laugh, but it's important to clue them in on the language you're using rather than spouting off jargon that you have yet to connect with course content. Don't assume anything. You don't want to end up looking like one of these:

C&I 13
When called on, students are given at least 5-10 seconds to formulate a response before asking someone else before you ask another student

You have the ability to transform the dynamics of your environment and promote active engagement during class discussions. Informing students in advance about their participation and sharing questions beforehand will empower them to prepare thoughtful responses, leading to deeper learning and enhanced critical thinking. Remember, effective communication and fostering a supportive environment are key elements in creating an optimal learning experience. So, take the initiative, implement these strategies, and witness the positive impact on your students' engagement and academic growth.

C&I 14
Teacher delivery rate of verbal language is slowed down but kept to a natural fluency

Slowing your pace down causes you to choose your words carefully and strategically. In and of itself, this is a great idea. You don't want any wasted language when working with your students.

Keep this in mind and record yourself reading the following speech in your "normal" teaching voice:

Ladies and gentlemen, boys and girls, today I want to take you on an exhilarating journey of discovery. Imagine a world where you have the power to shape your own destiny, where your ideas become the driving force behind change. Yes, I'm talking about the extraordinary realm of creativity. Whether you're doodling in the margins of your notebook or composing a heartfelt poem, creativity has the power to unlock hidden talents and unleash your imagination. It's a superpower we all possess, waiting to be unleashed. So, embrace your uniqueness, let your ideas soar, and remember, the world is your canvas. Together, let's paint a masterpiece of creativity!

<u>Now listen to your recording and jot down some notes about your:</u>
Rate:

Tone:

Prosody (expression):

Anything else you noticed:

C&I 15
Listening time" is segmented into shorter timeframes
Listening and *doing* are different things.

To keep your students engaged, break up your lessons into activities that include partner talks, independent learning, and group work. This will help all students engage with the content in a variety of meaningful ways.

THINK ABOUT IT
About what percentage of a typical lesson is spent:
Listening- _____
Doing- _____

This will look different depending on the age and subjects you teach, so use hte bottom of this page to reflect on each.

C&I 16
Verbal instructions are reinforced through repetition

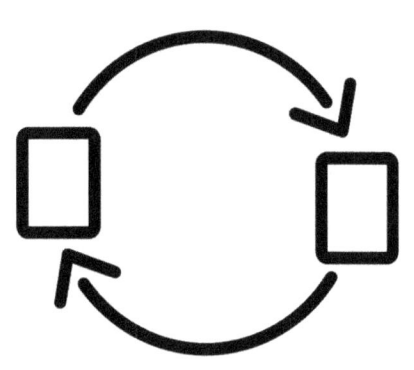

It can be helpful to gauge students' understanding/retrieval of your instructions, especially for those who may need reinforcement. You can ask them to summarize the instructions or repeat them back to you. In addition, you can reinforce verbal instructions by writing them on the board or having pre-prepared lists of instructions/items ready to share with your students. This can provide visual reinforcement and help ensure all students understand your expectations.

Reflection Notes:

C&I 17
Strategies and advice from speech language therapist/communication specialists are implemented with fidelity

Speech/language therapists and communication specialists are valuable resources for supporting neurodiverse students. They are experts in their field and are often willing to share strategies and supports that work. Consider asking them to come and model how they might support students with different needs in their area(s) of expertise. By acknowledging and valuing their capabilities, you can form highly effective collegial relationships, and they will know they have an ally in you. This collaboration can help ensure your students receive the best possible support and access to resources.

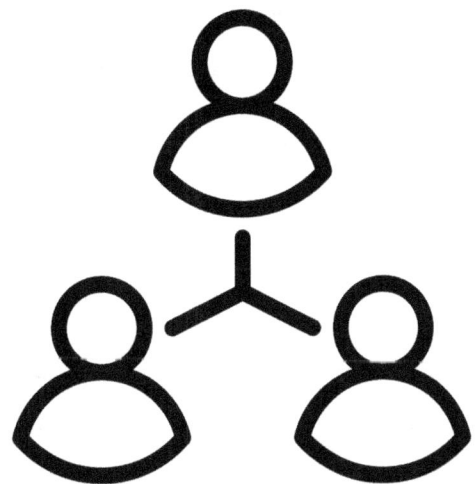

TAKE STOCK
List the therapists and/or designated "specialists" in your setting (e.g. it's OK if you don't know their name):

Make a plan to speak with them to help you support your neurodiverse learners and for those with communication differences. What questions do you have for them?

REFLECTION: COMMUNICATION & INTERACTION

Take a few minutes to review the 17 C&I Key Strengths for neurodiversity and inclusion, and answer the following questions:

Which 3 Key Indicator(s) do you believe are your strengths?
1. _____
2. _____
3. _____

Which 3 Key Indicator(s) could you target for development?
1. _____
2. _____
3. _____

How do you plan on maximizing each of these in your environment's daily routines?
_____
_____
_____
_____

How will you support others' development of their learning environment for C&I?
_____
_____
_____
_____

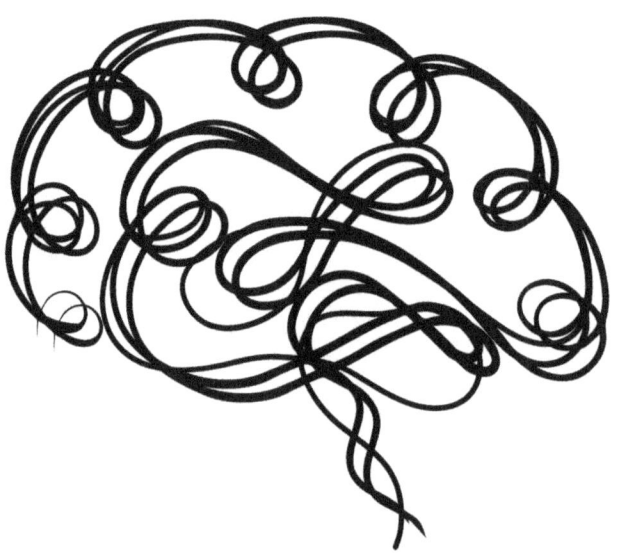

> How wonderful it is that nobody need wait a single moment before starting to improve the world.
>
> —Anne Frank

DEEP DIVE
LEARNING & COGNITION

Learning & Cognition (L&C) Warm-up

Reflect on what learning looks like and sounds like in your classroom. Note at least 5 observations for each question below.

What does it look/sound like for students who need additional support with learning class/lesson content?

1. _____
2. _____
3. _____
4. _____
5. _____

Think of 5 ways you believe your students with neurodiversities learn best:

1. _____
2. _____
3. _____
4. _____
5. _____

LEARNING & COGNITION PATHWAYS

Neurodiverse & Inclusive Learning Environments take into account the learning and cognition differences of all students. In this section, you will encounter a series of NAILEP Strength statements that serve as guiding principles for creating an environment that celebrates neurodiversity and fosters the growth of every student, regardless of their cognitive abilities. By embracing these strengths and applying them diligently to your teaching practice, you will establish a learning environment that acknowledges and respects the diverse learning needs of all students. Through this approach, you will empower your students to flourish and unlock their full potential.

L&C 1
Students are taught (and know) how to sequence skills, ideas, and work production

Not all students grasp sequencing naturally, leading to challenges in following directions, completing assignments, and expressing ideas verbally. To assist students in overcoming these learning differences, direct instruction of sequencing skills and ideas is highly beneficial. Here are some strategies to consider for supporting their success in creating meaningful learning products and completing assignments:

Engage in sequential or rhythmic games for valuable learning experiences. Traditional board games work for all ages and provide opportunities to learn turn-taking, planning, strategy, reasoning, and resilience.

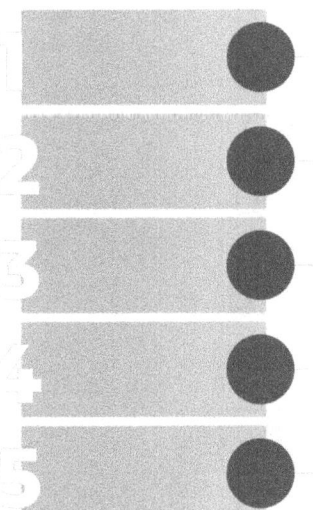

Provide task analyses or "recipes" for class, small group, or individual activities that require multiple steps. This can go on students' desks or on a board, and they apply to routines such as lunchtime or writing assignments, or any other complex task. Clear scripts help alleviate students' cognitive load, allowing them to focus on successfully completing the task.

Collaborate with parents when their child struggles with sequencing. Address concerns promptly to involve parents in providing support and fostering their child's success. While you cannot diagnose, you can recommend various strategies to enhance this crucial skill.

Write down 5 steps involved for learning how to ride a bike

Write down 5 steps involved for solving long division

L&C 2
Newly introduced vocabulary are pre-taught (or given to students) prior to initial instruction to ensure grasp of concepts/ideas discussed

Understanding a speaker who uses unfamiliar words and phrases can be highly confusing. Sitting through a lecture on a topic like quantitative easing without prior comprehension of the related terminology would be challenging.

Hence, when introducing new concepts, it is essential to allocate sufficient time (ideally several days) for students to learn and become familiar with new vocabulary through pre-teaching and direct instruction. Encouraging students to practice with their families and peers outside the classroom further enhances their understanding.

PLAN FOR IT
What are some vocabulary words you will teach in the near future? Think about some strategies you can use to pre-teach these:

L&C 3
Staff know the readability level of the text you expect students to read

"Readability level" refers to the calculated difficulty of a text, based on either age or grade-level norms. There are several formulas available to determine this, and each will provide an estimate of the difficulty level.

Online text

For online texts, you can determine the readability level by copying and pasting the text into *www.readabilityformulas.com* which provides seven different formulas. The text in this section is rated between 9th and 11th grade. However, it is important to note that you need to include a minimum of 100 words to get an accurate readability level.

Text from a book

If students are reading from a textbook, you will need to type 100 words from the text to obtain an accurate readability level. This may take a minute or two, but it will help you identify why students might struggle with certain texts. New camera phone technologies may allow you to circumvent the typing of words into the readability box.

L&C 4

When new ideas are introduced, they are explicitly connected to previously learned or understood concepts and events

Don't dismiss KWL Charts (Know- Want to know – want to Learn) as outdated. They are timeless and useful for helping students make connections and comprehend new learning. When introducing new concepts, it is important to explore the connections students might have to their learning. This creates a solid foundation on which they can build new knowledge and ask questions to expand it further.

What I already know	What I want to know	What I learned

L&C 5
Students are shown multiple ways to develop their knowledge and skills

Whether you are a traditionalist or an innovator, Universal Design for Learning (UDL) will help improve your teaching and classroom management. UDL considers how the brain interprets, processes, and demonstrates newly learned concepts and ideas. According to the Center for Applied Special Technology, or CAST (2018), teaching using a UDL framework allows for multiple ways for teachers to engage students, represent information to them, and provide opportunities for students to express and apply their new learning, leading to deeper understanding.

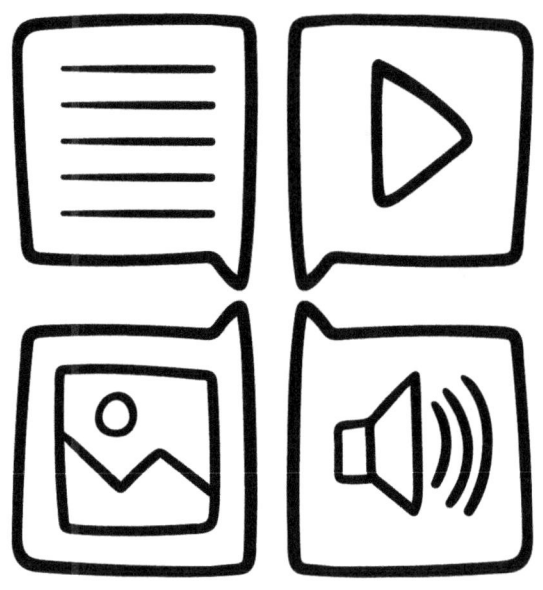

CAST (2018). Universal Design for Learning Guidelines version 2.2. Retrieved from http://udlguidelines.cast.org

PLAN FOR IT
What are some previous/upcoming projects or assignments you can give students different/creative options to communicate their learning?

L&C 6
Newly introduced items are reviewed during a lesson

Intentionality reigns supreme. Use newly introduced terminology throughout a lesson to help students develop their schema. While repetition alone may not be the most effective teaching method, it is important for building fluency. Fluency is comprised of rate, accuracy, and expression, and can be developed through intentional repetition.

L&C 7
Student skills and knowledge are assessed using different mediums and methods (e.g., written reports/essays, diagrams, mind maps, debates, voice recording, video presentations, etc.)

For over a century, schools predominantly relied on paper and pencil tasks, and occasional oral presentations to measure students' mastery of concepts, however, with the advent of technology and a renewed focus on resilience and character, new avenues have opened up for measuring individual and collaborative achievement. Here are a few alternative methods for measuring progress:

Written Reports: These provide students with a platform to showcase their learning progress, achievements, and writing skills to teachers and parents. They help students identify their strengths and weaknesses, set goals, develop reasoning skills, and improve academic performance. Written reports also serve as a record for future reference and evaluation.

Diagrams: Diagrams help students visualize and simplify complex ideas and concepts, making them easier to understand and remember. They aid in the development of critical thinking skills, enabling students to interpret information and present it to new audiences. Diagrams also enhance creativity, communication skills, and provide students with new methods to effectively express their ideas and thoughts. These diagrams might resonate with you and/or your students in meaningful ways and can be helpful for arranging and communicating learning:

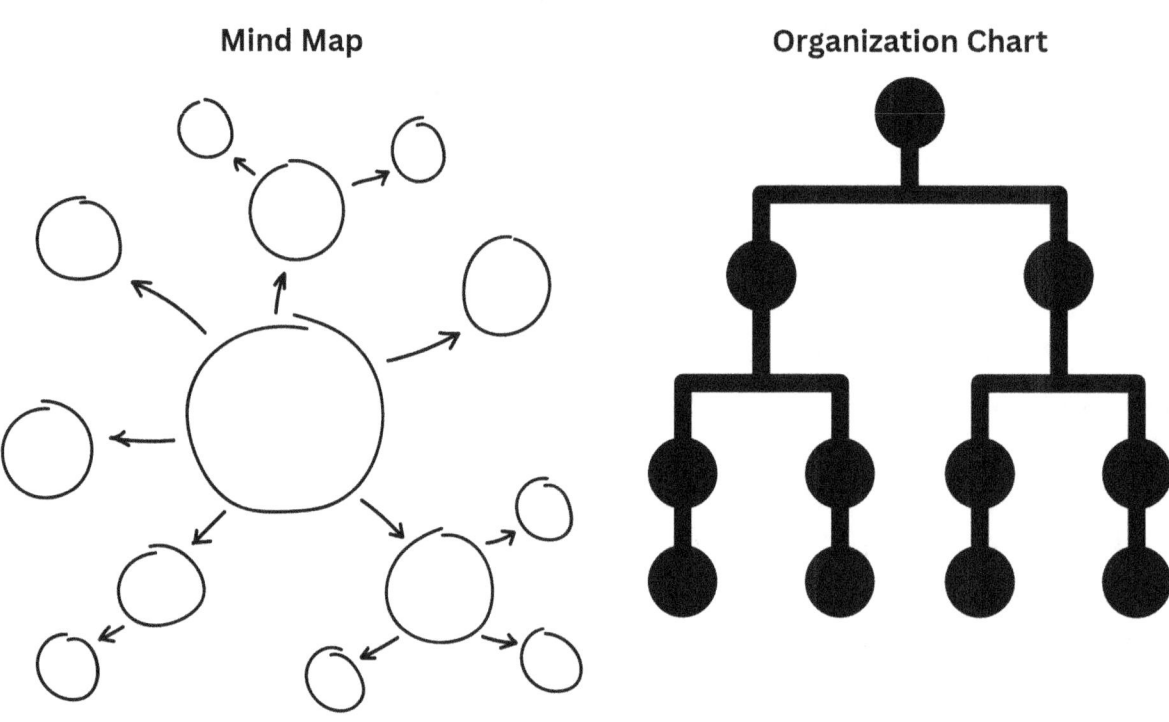

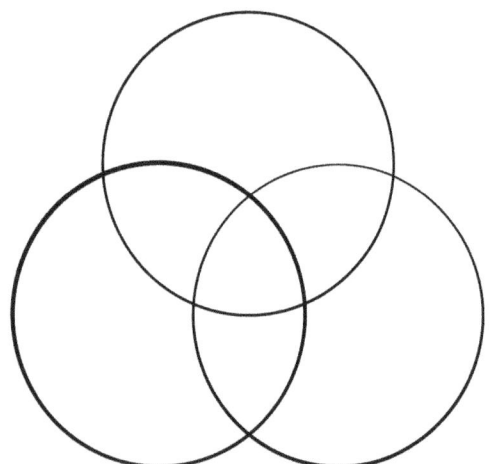

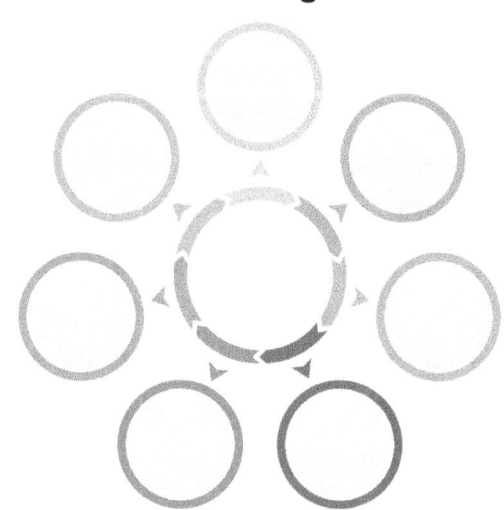

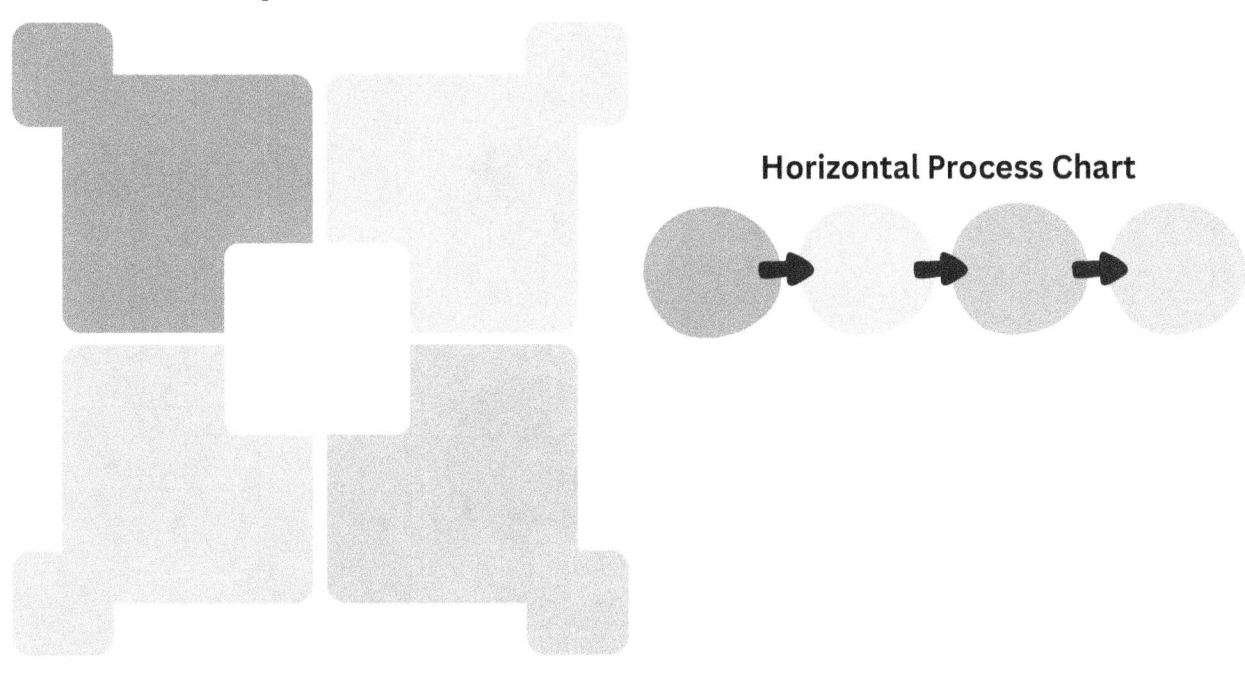

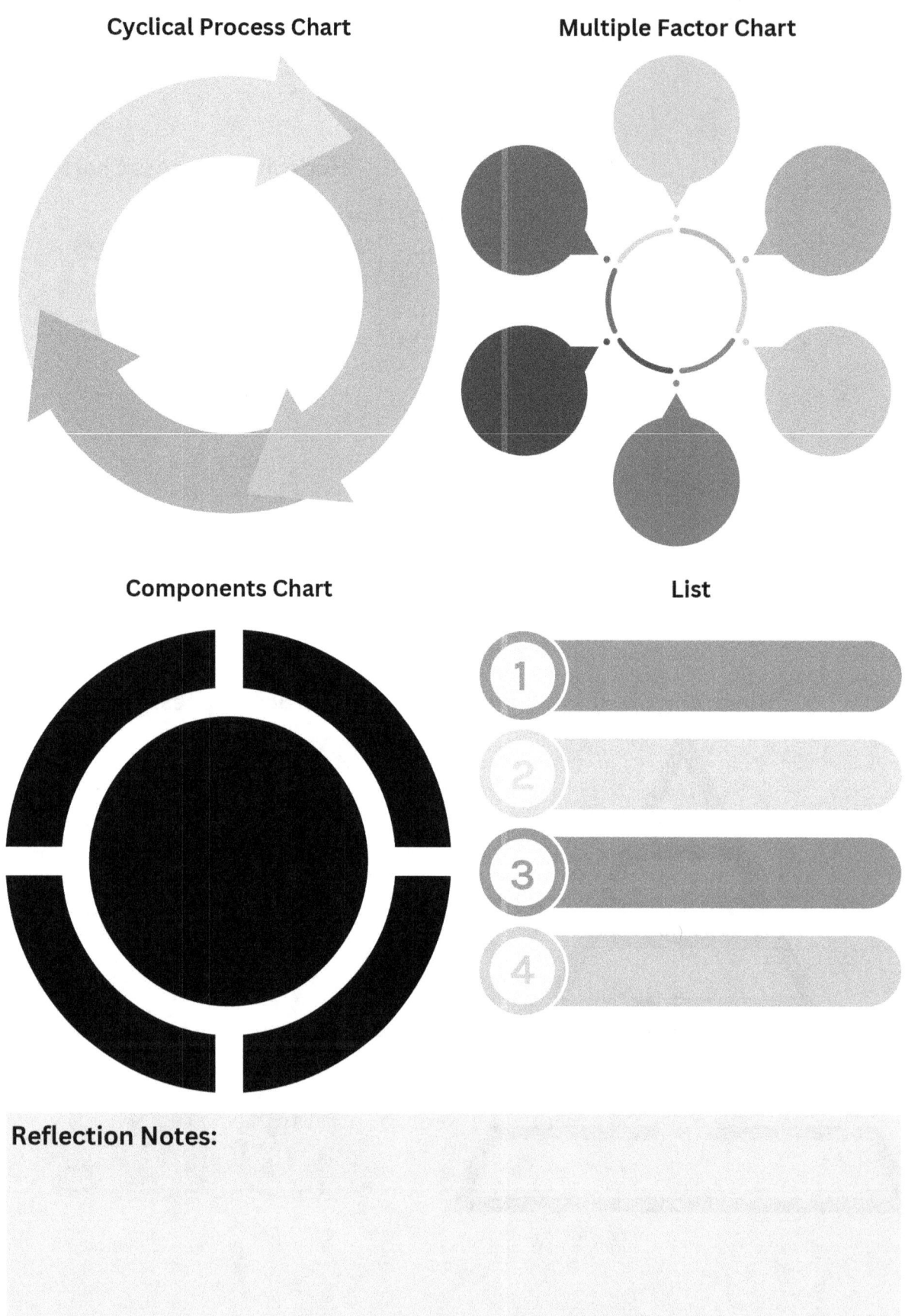

Mind Maps: Mind maps facilitate the organization and visualization of ideas. These color-coded maps promote creativity, critical thinking, and allow students to see how concepts and ideas are connective to form creative visual summaries of complex ideas. Mind maps can also serve as excellent study aids.

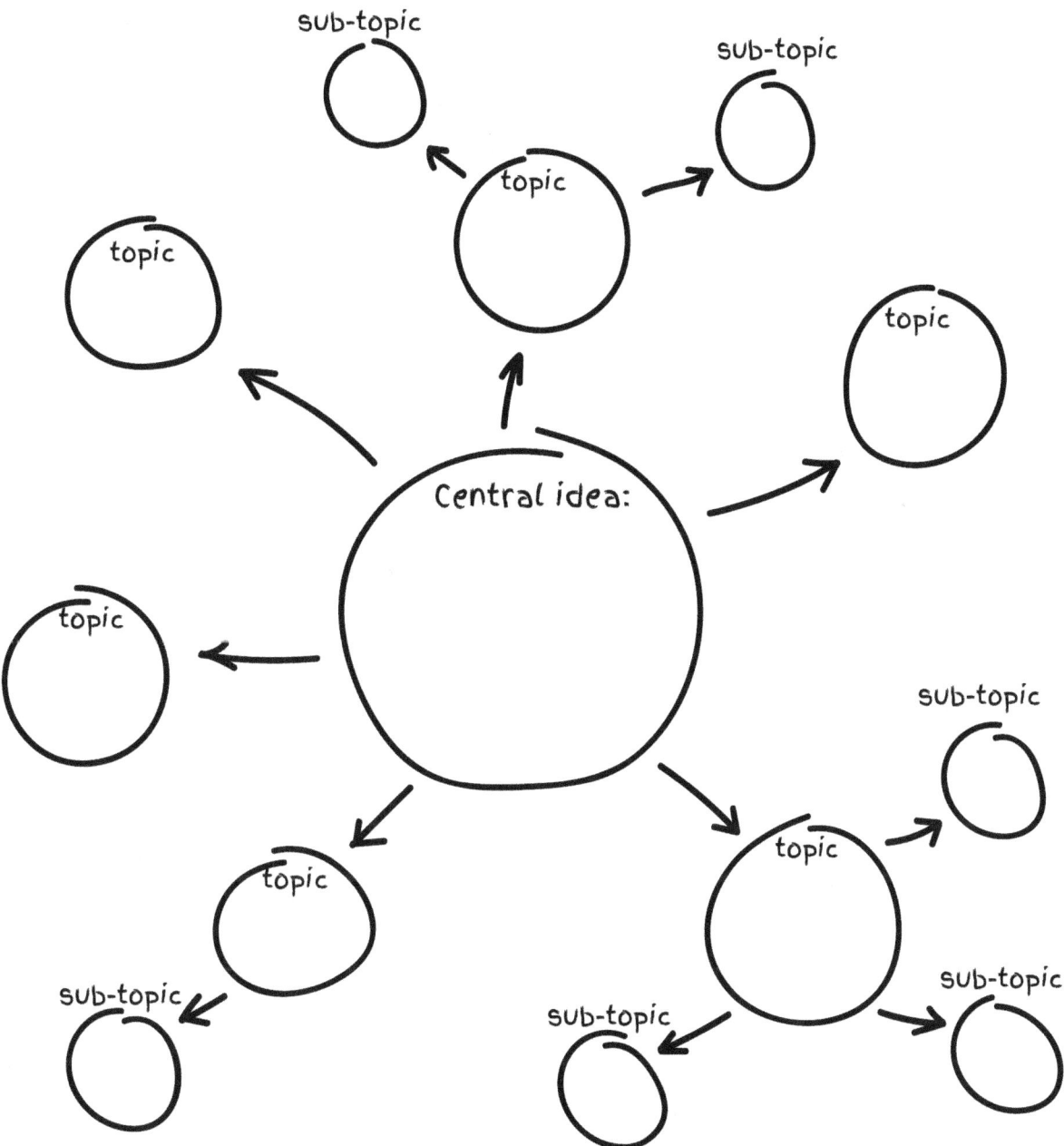

Remember, the purpose of a mind map is to visually represent information in a non-linear and interconnected way, stimulating creativity, and facilitating efficient information retrieval. Adapt the process to suit your preferences and needs.

Debates: Few methods are better for developing critical thinking, public speaking, and research skills than debates. Students have the opportunity to express their ideas persuasively while listening to others' viewpoints to gain a deeper understanding of differing perspectives.

Voice Recording: Voice recordings are not only useful assessment tools for teachers, but they can be highly effective self-assessments for students. Listening to recordings can help students improve pronunciation, fluency, and confidence. They can also learn to produce and edit information, a useful skill for various creative industries including media and entertainment.

Video Presentations: Video presentations help students develop digital fluency skills for the 21st century. Students learn to visually convey ideas and create engaging and meaningful content. This can be done independently or collaboratively, and students learn to express themselves and think critically by planning, creating, and editing their videos.

L&C 8
Class resources are grouped according to their kind and labeled with both words and symbols

Classrooms can be chaotic, and your resources often end up in strange places, are inadvertently destroyed, and can end up in the back of a student's desk or at the bottom of their bookbag. The best way to prevent this is by creating clearly labeled locations for all classroom items and by consistently reinforcing their use. This approach benefits neurodiverse students by providing a predictable and structured learning environment that fosters confidence When neglected order and systems can quickly spiral out of control, so remain vigilant about maintaining classroom organization to avoid unnecessary stress or complications.

L&C 9
All students are given the opportunity to use writing frames, flow charts, or rubrics to aid the organization of their writing for written assignments, narratives, essays, etc.

Previously, tools such as writing frames, flow charts, and rubrics were considered accommodations solely for students with individualized education plans (IEPs). However, these are now recognized as helpful for *all* students. Writing frames offer structures that many students will find useful, while flow charts assist students in organizing their writing for a more cohesive product. Rubrics display the skills and criteria students must demonstrate to excel in their writing, and they serve as useful teaching and assessment tools.

L&C 10

Key vocabulary terms are provided as handouts and color-coded into concept groupings so individuals can make connections to the main ideas learned

One way to make concepts more accessible to neurodiverse learners is by color-coordinating items to enhance connections. This quick-win strategy can support learners':

Retention: Learners have a greater likelihood of retaining information when they see it associated with other related concepts. Visual, colored discrimination of terminology groupings can aid in memory of the key ideas.

Understanding: Color-coding helps learners see the connections between concepts more easily, leading to a better understanding of the topic

Engagement: Learners are more likely to engage with visually appealing materials, which can lead to a more positive learning experience

Active Learning: Neurodiverse learners can highlight, take notes, and make annotations to add to learning engagement.

Reflection Notes:

L&C 11

Writing is graded for *grammar* using a rubric that all students have access to prior to and during written work

Having a shared language with grammatical standards is essential for enabling students to communicate effectively and eloquently through their writing. Teaching and assessing grammar empowers students to construct narratives and written products that are clear, concise, and coherent. It also enhances their ability to analyze and appreciate various types of literature and language. Rubrics can assist students in identifying specific steps they can take to enhance their grammar, based on either grade-level standards or a set of skill criteria in a rubric. See the example below.

L&C 12

Writing is graded for *content* using a rubric that all students have access to prior to and during written work

Teaching students how to write content that is relevant, informative, and engaging, as well as logical and well-organized, is a skill that requires artistry. Rubrics that outline the points awarded for the quality of content expected in a piece of writing will support neurodiverse learners with identifying and quantifying the skills they need to demonstrate for success.

			Sentence Score Sheet		
POINTS:	1	2	3	4	TOTAL
My response	No response	I wrote 1 word or 1 phrase	I wrote 1 complete sentence	I wrote more than 1 complete sentence	
Spelling	No words spelt correct	Half or less than half spelt correct	More than half spelt correct	All words spelt correct	
Mechanics	No capitalisation or final punctuation	Either initial capitalisation or final punctuation correct	Both initial capitalisation and final punctuation are correctly used	More than 1 sentence with: **Capital letters:** - beginning of sentences - proper nouns - names **Punctuation:** - at end of sentences	
Grammatical structure	Multiple grammatical errors that affect meaning or response is not a sentence	Some grammar correct- More than 1 error that does not affect meaning	Almost all grammar correct- 1 error that does not affect meaning	ALL grammar correct- no errors	
Did I follow instructions	Unrelated to the prompt	Related to the theme or idea	Response directly related but without elaboration	Direct relation to prompt and elaboration of writing	
				Total Score:	

L&C 13
Scribing for students (writing for them) is rarely used unless it is an accommodation provided for that student

Scribing for a student can be stigmatizing and create learned helplessness, so it should be avoided unless absolutely necessary. Here are a few reasons why:
- It may not address the root of the problem
- It is not feasible across settings
- It will likely be over-used

The best way to use a scribe is to have a student dictate what they want to write, but to scaffold this so they write various words/letters. Ultimately, the decision to use a scribe should be made on a case-by-case basis and you should work closely with all specialists who support the student to determine the most appropriate supports.

L&C 14
Students know how to use short-term memory-aids (e.g., markerboards, recording devices, etc.) and are given these if needed

Memory aids allow all learners to be more productive during lessons. Students will spend less time trying to retrieve information from numerous sources and can instead focus on the task at hand. This reduces what is known as cognitive load – the amount of information that working memory can hold at one time. Teaching students how to use these aids promotes independence and self-reliance – key resiliency skills they will need to be successful in life.

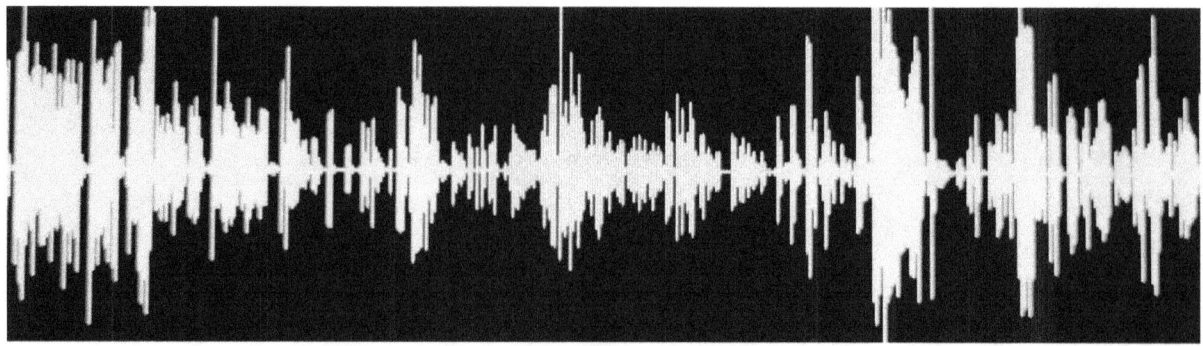

L&C 15
Printed materials are presented on off-white (cream or light pastel colored) paper and presented content is presented on a non-white background i.e., the screen/projector background is off-white)

Off white paper or backgrounds can alleviate eye strain caused by high-contrast black and white materials. Pure white paper can produce glare, which can be particularly vexing for some students. This can improve fluency and engagement with the content/materials presented.

L&C 16
Specific subject area books are available for all readability levels, regardless of the age being taught

Although sourcing textbooks and materials at every student's readability level will be difficult to come by- particularly with older students, there are small changes and adaptations you can make to portions of text using online sources.

Visit www.readabilityformulas.com to try it out!

L&C 17
Students have access to and/or are provided with "reading rulers" to help them keep their place on a page

Some learners struggle reading printed materials. One non-obtrusive tool found in neurodiverse and inclusive learning environments are reading rulers. These are transparent strips or bars with a colored tint (often yellow) used to help readers with visual processing difficulties, including dyslexia. The colored tint can reduce visual stress and make text easier to read. They also guide readers along each line of text which can improve focus and increase reading accuracy. Reading rulers come in different sizes and are often used by adults and children alike.

L&C 18
Presented materials (e.g., PowerPoint, displays) are uncluttered

Including too much information on slides must be avoided. In his humorous and informative TEDx Talk *"How to Avoid Death By PowerPoint,"* David JP Phillips offers valuable advice on how to create engaging presentations for your audience. Some his recommendations include:

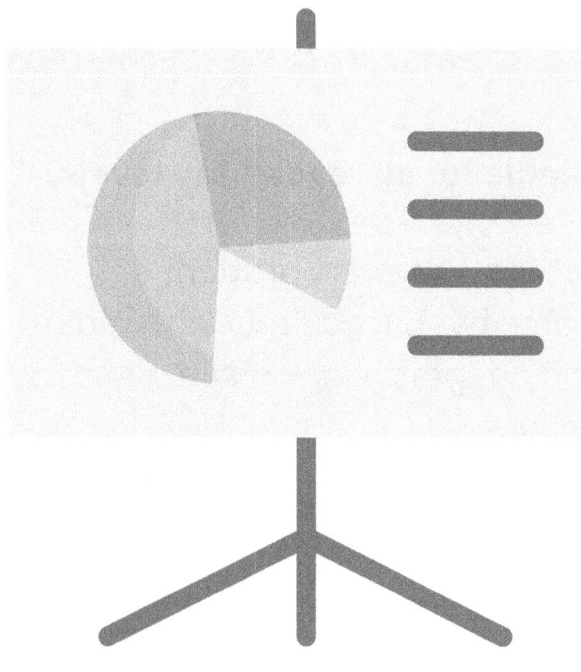

- Avoid cluttered examples, as 90% of what you say will be forgotten within 30-seconds
- Each slide should communicate one simple message
- Avoid redundancy by not writing everything you say on your slides
- Keep it concise, add an image that reinforces the main idea, and make sure the most important information stands out
- Reduce cognitive load by limiting each slide to six or fewer items
- Remember that it's not about the number of slides you use, but how many objects you put on each slide that can lose your audience's attention

TAKE A MOMENT
Watch the TEDx Talk "How to Avoid Death By PowerPoint," by David JP Phillips. Note some reflections here.
_____
_____
_____
_____
_____
_____

L&C 19
Presented materials (e.g., PowerPoint, displays) are high contrast to support visual discrimination

Following on from David JP Phillips's TEDx Talk "How to avoid death By PowerPoint", keep in mind that your slides should be visually appealing. This does not mean that you need to include fancy designs, but it does mean:
- Your eyes will focus on traffic signal colors like red, orange, and yellow
- Your audience will focus on big objects on a slide
- Slide title is often the biggest element of your slide but the least important
- Emphasize the major points you want to make with larger, contrasted text
- Use contrast to control your audience's attention
- Don't use light backgrounds! These steal too much attention from the presenter
- Use dark backgrounds with light text.

L&C 20
Diagrams and images add meaning to the text presented
To avoid death by PowerPoint, include images and diagrams that communicate your message better than words. This may require some creativity, but it will greatly benefit both you and your students.

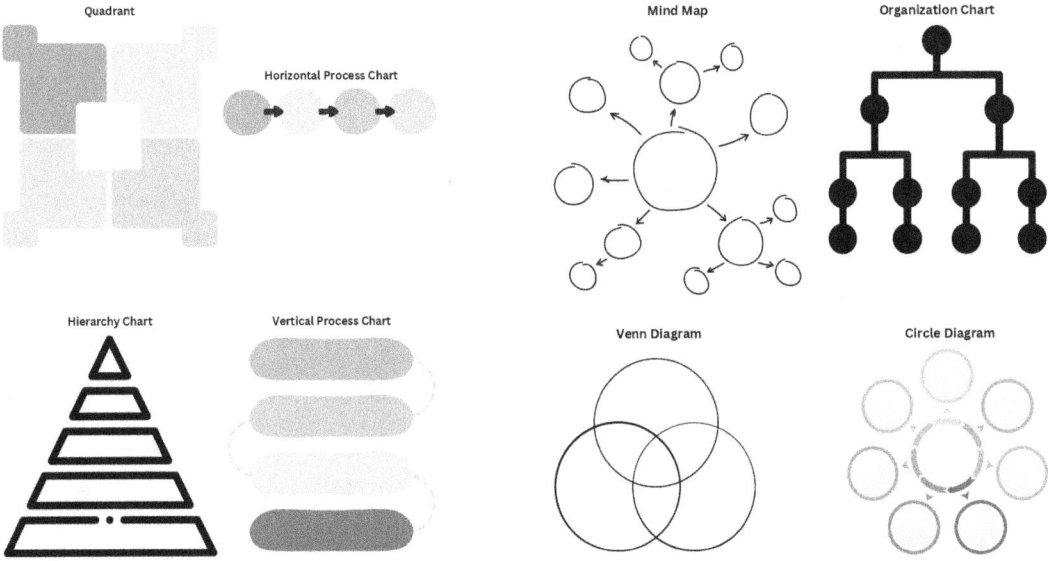

L&C 21
Students are given additional time to complete tasks

This simple environmental accommodation can be easily adopted to support all students, including those with processing differences, those who require organizational support, and those who value reviewing their learning products prior to submitting them. Additional time also gives all students the space to demonstrate what they know, regardless of time constraints. While deadlines are important, neurodiverse environments consider whether or not these are always suitable for all learners.

THINK ABOUT IT
Write down some of your students' names and about how much extra time you think they need to complete assigned projects or tasks. Think about building this time into your routines

_____
_____
_____
_____
_____
_____

L&C 22
Students use memory/mnemonic techniques that have previously been taught and modeled

Acronyms like "ROY G. BIV" for remembering the colors of the rainbow, and BEMDAS for mathematical processes are helpful for neurodiverse students from upper elementary to advanced mathematics. Other memory aids include:

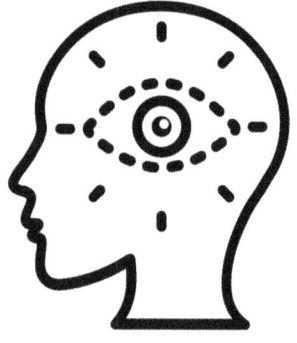

Visualization: Learners can create mental images to help remember information. For example, if they need to prepare for an assignment, spend some time beforehand helping them visualize what they will need and where in the learning environment they will retrieve these items. Another name for this could be "conscious planning".

Rhyming & Meter: Factual information is much better memorized with the use of rhyme and meter. Meter refers to a "beat" or a "pulse".

Chunking: When we break down information into smaller and more manageable pieces, we have a better chance memorizing it. Think of memorizing a phone number by chunking it into small groups of 3 or 4 numbers at a time (e.g., 989-555-1049).

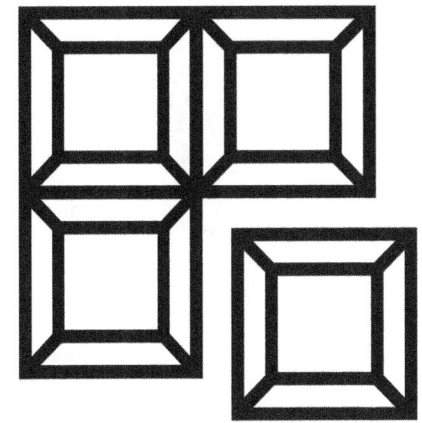

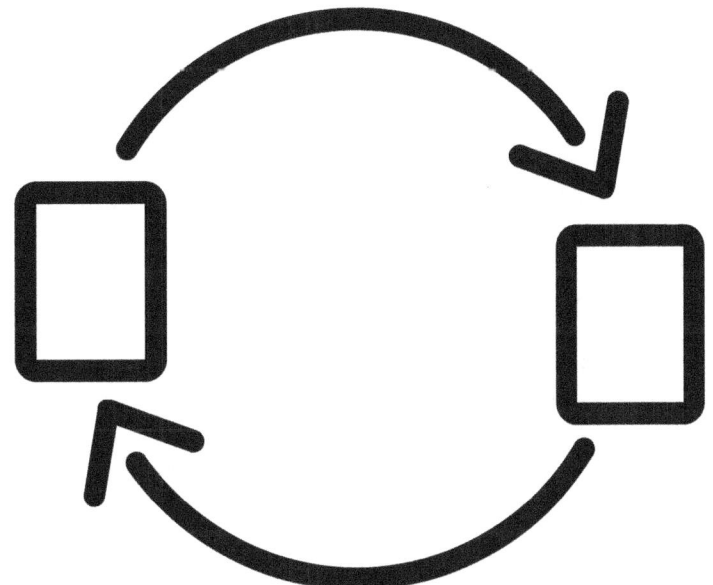

Repetition: Repetition is a strategy that has come up… repeatedly! This is because it can help your neurodiverse learners develop skill fluency. When you use these strategies, make sure you guide students through repeated practice so they can familiarize themselves with each and choose those that work best for them.

L&C 23
Copying from the board is kept to a minimum or avoided altogether – individuals have copies of presented or displayed materials at their desk for immediate access

Copying from the board, although once a common practice, has become less prevalent in modern teaching. However, it is important to consider why this practice is still used and its possible impact on students. For many students, copying from the board requires good short-term memory and motor processing skills, which may be difficult for neurodiverse students. This can result in a loss of focus and time that would have been better spent learning and understanding the actual content. Copying from the board also hinders critical thinking skills as learners become focused solely on transcribing the content. One solution to this is to provide localized copies of the content for students to keep in their learning space(s). this approach will not only reduce or eliminate the need for copying from the board but will also allow students to focus their attention on understanding the materials rather than recreating it, which will ultimately improve their learning outcomes.

L&C 24
Students are encouraged to explain assignments to others and/or teachers to check for understanding

It is important to resist the temptation to quickly give an assignment and expect immediate independence from all students. Neurodiverse learners possess countless skills, and when fostered in the right environment, will thrive. An effective approach is to perform a simple self-check for understanding prior to students beginning an assignment. This can be done in a variety of ways, including corporately with the whole class, in small groups, or 1:1 with students. By encouraging them to explain an assignment to others or to check with their teacher for understanding, educators can ensure that all students have a solid grasp of the material and feel confident in their ability to complete an assignment.

Working through the framework below will help you putting this in place:

The assignment is:_____

I know I will be successful if I: _____
_____
_____ _____

If I get stuck, I will: _____

I know I will be finished when:
_____ _____

When I'm finished I will: _____

L&C 25

Feedback "systems" are in place to help students know if they understand a concept or idea

If the ultimate purpose of feedback is to improve a student's performance, your systems can enable this. Here are a few that you can establish to ensure maximum impact of these systems:

Rubrics: As an assessment and student guide, rubrics are essential in the learning environment and can become part of the "system" when used regularly. The ultimate goal is for students to expect these and to independently access on a regular basis. L&C 12 has an example of a rubric, and you can create these for different subject and projects.

Peer Reviews: With a systematic and tactful approach, students can review and comment on one another's work.

Exit Tickets: Exit tickets have become increasingly popular in recent years due to their ease of use and simplicity These brief end-of-lesson assessments can take the form of surveys, quizzes, or reflections, and allow students to demonstrate their knowledge of the content.

Tech-Ins ("check-ins"): The availability of technology has made monitoring growth and progress easier in many ways. Software programs provide instructional support and evaluation tools to measure student mastery of skills, which can be used regularly to provide real-time feedback for teachers, neurodiverse learners, and their families

L&C 26
Students are encouraged to Turn & Talk at multiple points throughout a lesson

As a teacher, implementing "Turn & Talk" in your classroom can have numerous benefits. Not only does it improve student engagement, but it also provides you with immediate feedback, can encourage active participation, promotes critical thinking, and increases collaboration. While it is easy to ask questions and wait for students to raise their hands, this traditional method often results in only a handful of students participating regularly. By incorporating Turn and Talk activities, you can provide all students with opportunities to discuss, ask questions, and share their ideas with their peers.

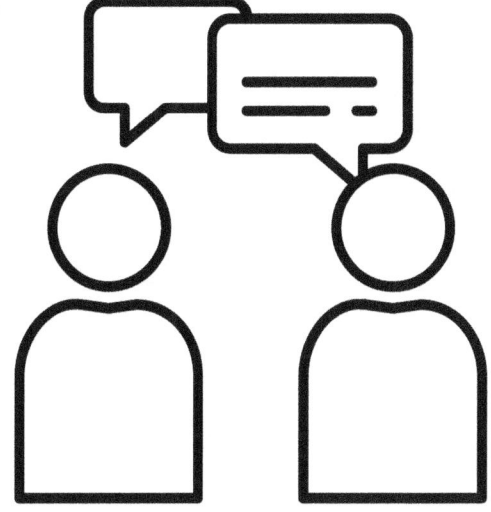

As the teacher, you can monitor both the knowledge and engagement of your students during these activities, making it an excellent form of formative assessment. Consider regularly incorporating this into your teaching routine and witness the positive impact it has on student learning and engagement.

Reflection Notes:

L&C 27
Parents are advised of new concepts and how they can support at home

Open communication with families empowers them to play an active role in their child's learning. This can create a healthy, collaborative learning community for neurodiverse students that leads to higher achievement and greater ownership. The benefits of these parent partnerships serve multiple purposes, including:

- Reinforcement of learning
- Collaboration with teachers
- Improved performance
- Communication and engagement

When we view students and their families as our partners and clients, we can enjoy finding new meaningful ways to support their learning beyond the school.

THINK ABOUT IT

How do you partner with families?

How do other colleagues partner with families that you think you can adopt?

What other ideas do you have to make parent partnerships more meaningful?

L&C 28

Metacognitive strategies are explicitly taught and encouraged (e.g., thinking out loud, if/then, I do this because, etc.)

Metacognition is the awareness and understanding of thought processes. In other words, it is "thinking about your thinking," and here is why this is a vital aspect of classroom learning:

Educators who show their neurodiverse learners how to pay attention to their thinking help students develop better study habits and reflection skills. This can lead to improved academic performance.

When shown how to use metacognitive skills to solve problems, learners can develop better critical thinking skills for talking themselves through problems

When neurodiverse learners better understand their own thinking, they can monitor progress and adjust the approaches and strategies they use, leading to more successful outcomes.

Students will ultimately develop confidence which leads to improved motivation for learning if they can identify the strategies and approaches that work for them and those that do not.

Reflection Notes:

REFLECTION: LEARNING & COGNITION

Take a few minutes to review the C&I Key Strengths for neurodiversity and inclusion, and answer the following questions:

Which 3 Key Indicator(s) are your greatest strengths?
1. _____
2. _____
3. _____

Which can you improve upon? How?
_____
_____
_____
_____
_____
_____
_____

How will you support others' development of their learning environment for L&C?
_____
_____
_____
_____

> It is not what you do for your children, but what you have taught them to do for themselves, that will make them successful human beings.
>
> –Ann Landers

DEEP DIVE
SOCIAL-EMOTIONAL STRENGTHENING

Social-Emotional Strengthening (SES) Warm-up

Before you read through the SES Pathway, consider the following:

How do you integrate SES into your (1) learning environment and curriculum, including (2) classroom instruction, (3) professional learning, and (4) school-wide policies?

1. _____
2. _____
3. _____
4. _____

How do you determine the effectiveness of SES programs/strategies, and what adjustments do you think needs to be made to these in your learning environment?

What we use:
_____
_____

How we measure:
_____
_____

Adjustments we can make:
_____
_____

What resources do we provide students and families with to support character and resilience at home and in the community?
_____
_____

What strategies do you personally use in your routines to support character and resilience in your environment?

_____ _____ _____
_____ _____ _____
_____ _____ _____

SOCIAL-EMOTIONAL STRENGTHENING PATHWAY

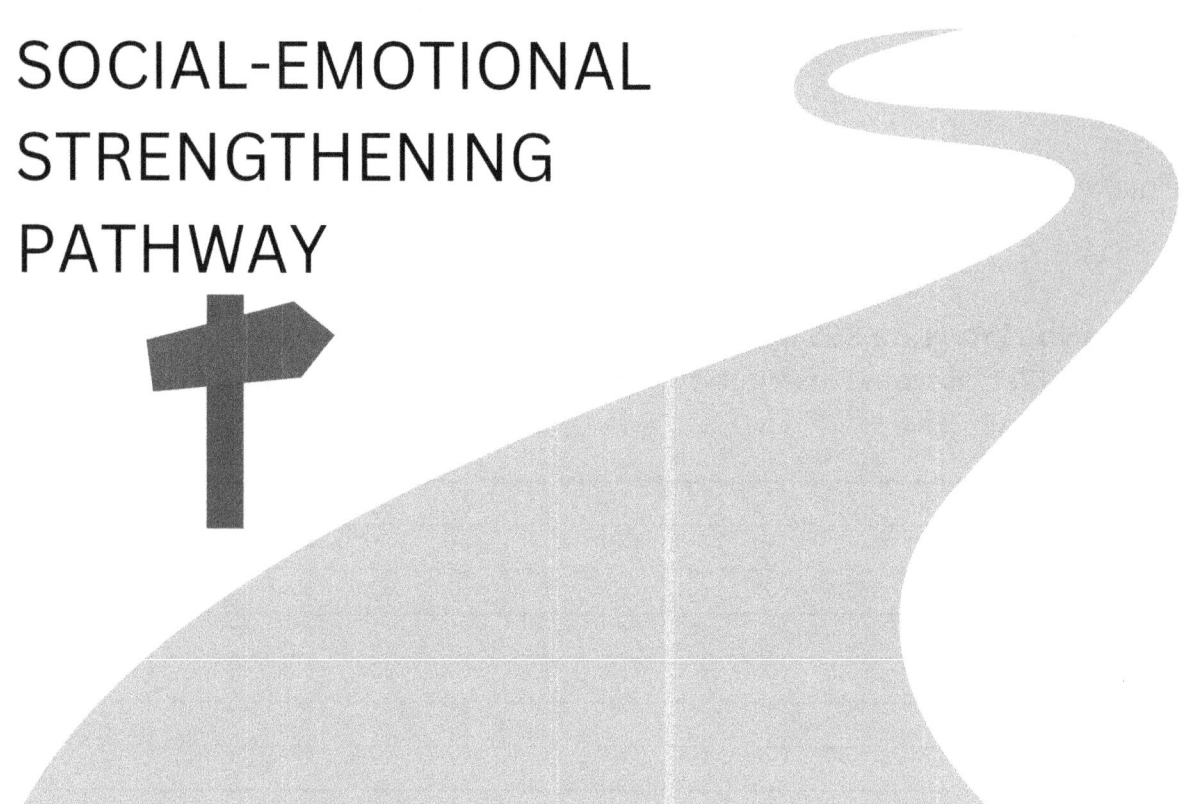

Social-Emotional Strengthening (SES) Pathway is the bedrock for developing independent, engaged, high-achieving learners who collaborate well. How well does the learning environment you have created serve to support the development of these skills? We will explore the SES Key Strengths and work together to make sure your students are supported in their character development through just, equitable, and consistently applied routines and procedures.

SES 1
While excellence and achievement are stated values in your learning environment, students know it's OK to not be perfect

Achievement is a vital aspect of school learning, but it is important to remember it is not synonymous with growth. Many mistakenly emphasize either-or, rather than both... but your learning environment must be different!

Healthy competition should be encouraged along with excellence in presentation, output quality, and other educational achievement factors. This does not negate the importance of praising growth but highlights the importance of each of these.

With that said, students need to know it's OK to not be perfect and embrace their imperfections; to see them as opportunities for growth and learning. By doing so, they develop resilience and growth mindsets which help them rebound from setbacks and challenges. People who understand it's OK to not be perfect are:

- More likely to seek help when they need it
- Open to feedback, constructive criticism, and redirection
- Empathetic and compassionate
- Recognize and value the *whole* person in others and themselves

Revisit page 20 and share and note any thoughts about your own mindset of growth and performance

SES 2
Students are praised for progress and growth, not just perfection

Praising students for progress and growth develops a positive attitude toward learning, builds resilience, and can reduce unnecessary anxiety. Here are four reasons to praise growth, not just perfection:

Fosters a love of the learning process- while outcomes are important, the process to achieving the outcomes is where depth of learning takes place

Creates confidence- students can develop confidence in their abilities, see themselves as capable of achieving goals, and they are likely take on new challenges

Growth mindset- students learn that their abilities and capabilities change and develop through resilience

Reduces stress and anxiety- while not all students have perfection anxiety, some do and become overly focused on getting everything right. Praising for progress and growth helps students feel valued for their earnest effort and reduces unhealthy perfectionism.

Do you have a propensity to encourage *growth* or *performance*? Provide some examples.

Growth:
_____
_____
_____
_____
_____

Performance:
_____
_____
_____
_____
_____

SES 3

Student groupings take into consideration individual strengths and how the group will work together to create a meaningful learning experience

If you know your students' strengths (via Strengths Explorer, StrengthsFinder, observation, etc.), you will have a firm understanding of how different strengths complement one another. Effective student groupings can:

Help them develop **collaborative skills** such as communication, respect, and relational intelligence

Encourage **active engagement** and participation from all students which can lead to a deeper understanding and a rich learning experience

Create a more **supportive environment** for neurodiverse learners by promoting communication between students

Each of these are essential to strengthen students' core responses.

SES 4
Students who need it sit closer to the source of instruction/delivery (e.g., the teacher, screen, etc.)

Sitting closer to the source can allow students to better see and hear presented information, which might improve both behavior and their comprehension of the content. While this is no guarantee, by doing so you reduce distractions from external stimuli which promotes focus.

SES 5
Students are given the opportunity to participate in meaningful real-life experiences or simulations

When we are intentional about connecting school curriculum and content to the real-world, we help students see connections beyond the four walls of our classroom. Emphasize this in order to:

- Create hands-on opportunities to reduce learning disassociation
- Improve collaboration skills through problem solving tasks and decision-making activities, communication skills
- Explore and analyze new perspectives and scenarios
- Develop social responsibility by exposing them to different cultures and mindsets
- Help students explore possible careers through real-life simulations that mimic possible career paths to determine whether a particular field is a good fit for them

Consider...

How you utilize hands-on opportunities to reduce learning disassociation

In what ways do you help students develop social responsibility through understanding different cultures?

How do you help students analyze new or different perspectives or scenarios?

How do you help students explore career paths and opportunities to demonstrate real-world skills?

SES 6
Social-emotional and character-building advice from specialist teams are followed

Educators have expertise in multiple areas of child development, curriculum subjects, instructional strategies, and much more. It is also important to acknowledge the expertise of those around you and to seek their advice when needed. Mental health professionals, specialists, and counselors who have training and expertise in areas of social-emotional strengthening and character development can provide valuable support for children and youth. Their advice can help you build the social-emotional and character-building skills needed to thrive in life beyond school.

Who are the specialists that support social and emotional strengths in your building or in the community?

What other relationships or interests do students have that you can leverage to help them succeed if they are having difficulties? Think of a few students and their abilities or interests...

SES 7

Precipitating factors are considered by classroom staff prior to engaging in academics (e.g., specific students requiring support are met at the door and given a moment to talk through any issues)

"Precipitating factors" are beyond your control. They include the challenges and issues a student faces prior to entering your learning environment that can lead to unproductive or even unpredictable behaviors. It's like if someone shook a can of soda without you knowing and then gave it to you. Sometimes, our students experience situations like this before entering the learning environment.

By meeting your students at the door, you can get a feel for the factors (e.g., emotions, behaviors, joys, troubles, etc.) they might bring into your school or classroom. This brief but intentional interactions will go a long way in building trust and can have lasting effects in the lives of the students you support.

SES 8

A student's strengths are made explicitly clear to them, and they are aware of these (e.g., through praise, StrengthsExplorer or other assessments/evaluations)

If you are not familiar with *StrengthsExplorer*, take a moment to look it up. It is an assessment for young people aged 10-14 that gives them a chance to discover their natural strengths at an early age. The assessment is quick and easy to complete, and it can help students and adults better understand a child's unique strengths. If you want to improve your teaching abilities and help your students reach their full potential, this is a valuable tool that will help your students develop their social-emotional strengths and find greater meaning in and out of school.

But why should your younger students have all the fun? *StrengthsFinder* is designed for those 15+ and provides similar reports for older students and adults. It's affordable and you will receive a high-quality report to highlight specific action points to help you capitalize on your personal strengths. If you are interested in learning how to teach with your strengths and understand those of the students you teach, take some time to complete the test.

Write down the inherent strengths or skills you see in some of your students. It's OK to be optimistic!

Student	Natural strengths
_____	_____
_____	_____
_____	_____
_____	_____
_____	_____
_____	_____

SES 9

Students have regular opportunities to develop their strengths through a variety of lessons

Some students naturally know their strengths while others need someone to help bring it out of them. By taking a vested interest in your students, you will discover more about their strengths and work with them to develop these. Your lessons and the assignments you give won't always be catered to their strengths – nor should they be – but it will help you understand the connections your students will make to the content and projects you assign. Make a chart like the one below to help you and your staff team better understand and support your learners.

> On the next page is a continuation of this chart that you can use to reflect on your students' strengths. Take some time to fill it in and talk with colleagues who also know the students. Consider the implications for what it means in your learning environment.

STUDENT	NATURAL STRENGTHS *Positive traits*	BARRIERS *What gets in the way*	STRATEGIES *What you can do*
Christopher	Performer/entertaining Caring/helping Relatable/makes friends easily	Timing not always appropriate Often misses class to care for friends Not everyone sees friendships similar	Help him identify appropriate times to respond Praise him in front of others People want to be around him

STUDENT	NATURAL STRENGTHS *Positive traits*	BARRIERS *What gets in the way*	STRATEGIES *What you can do*
Christopher	Performer/entertaining Caring/helping Relatable/makes friends easily	Timing not always appropriate Often misses class to care for friends Not everyone sees friendships similar	Help him identify appropriate times to respond Praise him in front of others People want to be around him

SES 10
Classroom staff are aware of specific social, emotional, and mental health needs, and relate to students in a way that empowers them to achieve their best

Teachers who understand students and see their strengths help set them up for success in and outside of the classroom. Teachers are not meant to be friends with students, but can guide them toward ambitious, achievable outcomes in school and beyond. Doing so builds character, compassion, resilience, and grit – key attributes that they will need to be successful.

SES 11
There are clear consequences and boundaries for student misbehavior, and staff follow through with stated consequences

If you and a friend go out to a large, blank, paved surface with no lines painted on the ground, two racquets and some tennis balls, but then your friend starts wildly hitting the ball all over the place and boldly proclaims "I WIN!" Would that be much of a tennis game? Of course not. Tennis requires a net, baselines, service lines, and sidelines. In this case, there were no rules, no boundaries, and no expectations for etiquette. Not good!

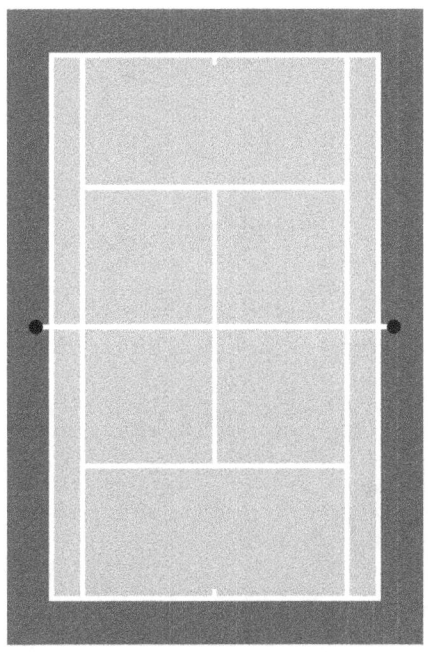

Your educational and classroom expectations – including the boundaries you set – should be predictable and consistently reinforced every day and in every lesson. Without it, your students and staff will quickly lose trust in you and your ability to follow through with what you say you will do. Too many teachers lose faith in their school leadership because of their unwillingness to enforce consequences or because no clear boundaries have been established. It is vital that families, teachers, and school leaders establish clarity and consistency through quality communication.

SES 12
Sanctions or discipline of any kind are not stated in a punitive manner (e.g., "I'm taking away…" or "I'm going to give you…"), but are stated in a way that discipline is a result of a choice the student made – "You chose to… so the consequence is…"

If you want students to resent you, tell them you're the giver and taker of their rights and privileges. If you want them to feel empowered and responsible, let them know their actions have both positive and negative consequences.

SES 13
Students know you like teaching them

I know what some of you are thinking: "I'm not here to be liked. I'm here to teach."

True, but here are a few keys to being a successful teacher:
1. Have a heart
2. Enjoy what you do
3. Enjoy who you do it with.

If these are hard for you, that's OK…

But you should find another job.

SES 14
Students are given breaks between tasks, including transition time between activities

Taking breaks between activities is important for maintaining productivity, creativity, and well-being. It can also help you avoid burnout and to work more efficiently through:

Reduced stress- breaks can help reduce stress by giving students time to relax

Rest and rejuvenation- breaks between activities give your body and brain time to regain focus

Enhanced creativity- breaks allow your thoughts to wander and provide space for your brain to make new connections

Improved productivity- short breaks throughout the day help you maintain focus and sustain performance

SES 15
Staff know what might trigger challenging behavior from students and have made environmental adaptations to minimize these

Teachers should know what might trigger challenging behavior to prevent or de-escalate difficult situations before they arise. This does not mean you should tip-toe around students, but when teachers understand environmental factors that contribute to negative behavior (e.g., triggers), they can proactively modify strategies to support behavior.

SES 16
Staff are aware of the positive peer relationships a student has, and helps them develop these through educational activities

We thrive best in community, and by knowing how our students relate with their classmates we can find new ways to make social learning a reality in class. Speak with families and your colleagues and take an interest in how your students relate to one another outside the classroom. Think of collaborative educational activities you can create to help your students do the following:

Improve knowledge	Develop their own learning goals	Access resources in and out the classroom	Show understanding of how working in a group promotes their learning	Display communal responsibility for the learning environment
Help one another through dialogue	Create products for themselves and others	Review how the community supports them	Show how classroom structures promote interdependence and community	Link new knowledge with prior learning (schema)

SES 17
A range of multi-sensory resources, stress-relieving and transition objects are available, and students have independent use of these, as needed

A number of retailers sell stress-relieving or transition objects, and you can find these on your favorite large retail site. If you teach elementary-aged students who have significant behavioral challenges while transitioning from one environment to another, you may want to introduce "transition objects". These are small, non-distracting, objects such as a little toy, or something small/soft and nice to touch. Think of this like a security blanket for older kids who have attachment difficulties. This certainly will not solve the difficulties associated with transitioning, but it often works and supports students with these challenges.

How to use a transition object:
1. When your student prepares to leave one learning environment, they retrieve their transition object from the designated location
2. The student prepares to leave the room with their class (i.e., they get in line or follow whichever routine is used)
3. They responsibly go to the new learning environment with their object in hand
4. When they enter the class, the new teacher helps them store their object in a designated location where they can see it from their seat or desk

Who are they for: Any student who feels worried, insecure, or acts out when transitioning from one physical location (room) to another.

Set-up: Establish a designated location in your environment and in other school learning environments where the student must "store" (or keep) his or her transition object while engaging in a lesson. It's best to keep this in a visible place near the doorway or entrance/exit to a classroom. This is a ground-rule and serves multiple purposes:
- Transitions become more predictable
- The object will not distract the student during a lesson
- Students develop independence
- You have created the circumstances in which these are used. You as a teacher are in control of the learning environment you created with clear expectations for behavior and relationships.

SES 18

Interactive strategies are used to engage students (e.g., students use cards and markerboards to hold up their answers in group lessons, students participate in role play, interactive tech tools, etc.)

Maybe it goes without saying, but deep learning does not take place by sitting and listening to someone talk about a topic or idea. The best learning must be experienced to be retained. It's true that facts can be memorized, but there are better ways to engage your students in real learning. Here's how.

Role-Play: By acting out scenarios, students can develop a number of skills including problem-solving, communication skills, deeper understanding, and synthesis of the learning.

Cooperative Learning: When students learn together to complete meaningful projects, they support one another's learning through the sharing of ideas and effective communication. This can have a lasting impact on deep learning.

Inquiry-Based Learning: This approach encourages students to ask and answer their own questions through investigation. In doing so, they can develop a deeper understanding of course content through critical thinking.

Gamification: When learning activities incorporate game-like elements like badges or short-term awards for completing tasks, creative teachers can find new and innovative ways to incentivize learning.

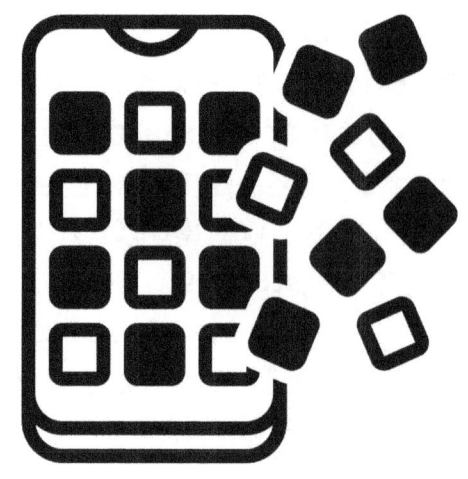

Technology: Apps, online resources, and interactive simulations are ways to leverage technology in the classroom

SES 19
Expectations for student behavior are explicit, achievable, and are made clear through student targets, explanation as needed, and adult or peer modeling

- Explicit expectations for standards of behavior reduce misunderstanding and ambiguity
- Modeling provides positive examples of your expectations where students first observe you and then take part demonstrating the expectation
- Achievable expectations build confidence through realistic, attainable targets that can build confidence
- Your consistency creates a stable learning environment where all students have the best opportunity to thrive

SES 20
Feedback to students is S.P.I.T.
- Feedback is *specific* to a skill demonstrated rather than a vague comment such as "good job"
- Feedback to students is *positive* – it builds on strengths
- Feedback to students is *instructional* – it provides direction related to a skill
- Feedback to students is *true* to what they have visibly demonstrated in their work

SES 21
Students know how to utilize physiological strategies to calm themselves

From the greatest E-suite executives to the classroom, the use of calming physiological strategies can help you and your students' self-regulation, and will allow you to make more powerful and effective decisions:
- Palms Up: Instead of clenching a fist, keep your palms open and faced upwards. The point is to not let your fingertips touch anything which can both increase tension and show frustration.
- Deep breathing: This can reduce feelings of anxiety and will lower your heart rate, allowing you to make more productive decisions. Here's how: Slowly inhale through your nose, hold for a few seconds, and then slowly exhale through your mouth. Repeat.
- Meditation: We often think of meditation as having to do with religion, but this does not always have to be the case. It can be around a positive experience, a deep thought, or to a relaxing song/recording.

SES 22
Staff are aware of how to personalize student learning in meaningful ways

When Ambitious Educators understand their students' backgrounds, experiences, and how to inspire learning in and outside the classroom, they can personalize learning in significantly meaningful ways. This entire neurodiversity and inclusion program is about making environmental changes to classroom routines, structures, and systems that work for you – not catering every aspect of your teaching to the 10-30 students in your class. That is impossible.

> **Ambitious teachers make environmental changes that reduce barriers so all learners can engage in meaningful learning. While understanding student interests can be a helpful tool to personalize lessons and aspects of learning, think big picture (i.e., systems and environment).**

SES 23
Rules and expectations are short, precise, instructional, and positively stated (e.g., We keep our property safe by putting it in our bag/locker)

The once-popular phrase "Keep it simple, stupid!" might be useful when considering your school or learning environment rules/covenants. The three best rules are Be Safe, Be Responsible, Be Respectful. As a teacher, you can break these down into explicit actions, but your rules should be anchored in one of these three statements. After teaching students about what this mean, they should be able to ask and answer the questions:
Is it Safe?
Is it Responsible?
Is it Respectful?

SES 24
Language used to address students is clear, calm, and respectful

Here's why your language (expressive and receptive) is important:
1. It promotes positive **relationships**: When you communicate clearly and calmly, you set the tone for how other adults and students should do so in a healthy environment
2. It models appropriate **behavior**: You model for students what a healthy, positive relationship looks like, even in conflict
3. It **reduces** anxiety: If a student is experiencing anxiety, more verbal language, including demands and commands, will only make it worse.

- To reduce anxiety and improve student autonomy when they are escalated, do the following:
- Do not show negative emotion
- Use fewer than 5 words
- Speak slowly and clearly
- Wait for a response by giving students 10-seconds before repeating the direction
- Repeat

SES 25
Students are given opportunities to discuss their behavior during or after a lesson

Problematic behavior should be discussed with a student once they are calm and able to have a conversation about it. Conversations should be structured and consistent so as to understand precipitating factors, antecedents, and consequences administered as a result.

A good way to begin conversations might be: "Tell me about..." or "Can you explain what happened...", rather than "Why did you..." or "Billy said you took his calculator..." The open ended, non-accusatory prompt is more likely to facilitate an honest answer. Other prompts you can use include:

- *Let's talk about...*
- *What are some examples of respectful/safe/responsible behavior...?*
- *What are some strategies you can use when...*
- *Why is it important to be aware of body language and tone when...*
- *What are some of our key classroom rules or covenants?*

The goal is to engage students in constructive reflection and conversation rather than being judgmental or accusatory.

> **THINK ABOUT IT**
> **What are some phrases or sentence starters you use with students that have proven to be effective?**

SES 26
Students know and can identify the positive features of their classroom culture

Neurodiverse and Inclusive learning environments have clear, identifiable, cultural features, and these are regularly reinforced communicated to students. They, in turn, are able to communicate this culture to their parents and peers.

Below you will read some positive statements. Respond to the statement with examples for what each looks like in your learning environment.

We work together to improve our knowledge	We are actively engaged in group conversations
We are curious and respectful about others' opinions	We act respectfully toward our classmates, adults, and property
How we respond is not dependent on anyone else. I am in control of myself.	We are not afraid to try new things
Learning takes place in everything we do	I have gifts and talents that can solve difficult problems

SES 27

Positive achievements are shared with parents on regular basis

Here are some ways that parents and teachers can partner together:

Celebrate success

When students succeed, it is important for parents and teachers to celebrate their accomplishments together. This can help to strengthen the bond between the student, their family, and their school.

How do you do this?

_____

_____

Create partnerships

Parents and teachers can build trust and a sense of partnership by sharing information about students' progress at home and at school. This can help to ensure that students are getting the support they need to succeed.

How do you do this?

_____

_____

Reinforce desired outcomes

Parents and teachers want students to learn the importance of dedication, achievement, perseverance, and dedication. Effective family partnerships can reinforce these character strengths by working together to set goals and track progress.

How do you do this?

_____

Provide constructive support.

When parents are valued members of an inclusive and neurodiverse community, they can provide constructive support at home to support their child's in-school learning. This can include providing a quiet place to study, helping with homework, and talking about the day's lessons.

How do you do this?

_____

Motivate students

When parents know about their child's in-school achievement, they can provide in-home motivation that improves their access to opportunity. This can include talking about the importance of education, setting goals, and providing encouragement.

How do you do this?

_____

_____

SES 28

Students are addressed by their name prior to giving a direction

When teachers address students by name, they acknowledge the student's presence and demonstrate that they are paying attention. This can help to create a sense of belonging and respect in the classroom. Additionally, addressing students by name can help to improve active listening. When students hear their name, they are more likely to tune in and pay attention to what is being said.

There are a few things to keep in mind when addressing students by name. First, it is important to pronounce the student's name correctly. Second, it is important to use the student's name in a respectful way. Finally, it is important to be mindful of the student's cultural background. In some cultures, it is considered disrespectful to address someone by their first name unless they have given you permission to do so.

- When giving instructions: "Sally, please raise your hand if you have a question."
- When praising students: "Great job, John! I really appreciate your hard work on that project."
- When redirecting students: "Michael, I need you to put your pencil down and listen to me."

This one small tactic helps create a positive classroom climate that is conducive to learning.

SES 29

Staff model the features of healthy, collegial relationships with one another, and students are aware of this

High-quality learning environments are built on respectful collegial relationships. These are the foundation of a positive school culture. They create a sense of community and support for teachers and students and provide neurodiverse students with the consistency and stability they need to thrive. Educational staff can build and model collegial relationships in the following ways:

- Get to know your colleagues. Take the time to learn about their interests, strengths, and challenges.
- Be supportive. Be there for your colleagues when they need help.
- Be respectful. Treat your colleagues with the same respect that you would want to be treated with.
- Be collaborative. Work together with your colleagues to solve problems and improve the school.

THINK ABOUT IT

Think about your workplace relationships. Do they model how you want your students to act, respond, or relate toward their peers? Feel free to reflect in this space.

Education leaders have a vital role in modeling this as well. Effective leadership creates a positive school culture that has:

Low turnover rate- A low turnover rate indicates that teachers are happy and supported at the school.

Engaged families- When families are engaged in their children's education, it creates a sense of community and support for the school.

Professional development opportunities- Professional development opportunities that are relevant to teachers' interests help them to feel valued and supported.

Collaboration between teaching teams and leadership to solve problems. When teachers and leadership work together to solve problems, it creates a sense of trust and respect.

SES 30

Students are aware of sabotaging behavior and are taught to adjust accordingly

Some neurodiverse students might not be aware how their behavior affects their relationships and learning, and it can be tempting as adults to try and save the day. Some common behaviors that neurodiverse students may exhibit include the items below. Make notes about what this might look like for students in your learning environment and how you can help students learn to receive and accept praise, compliments, and responsibility.

Refusal to attempt tasks

Avoiding people, places, or activities

Self-degradation

Withdrawing from others

Complaining of illness to get out of assignments

Deflecting compliments

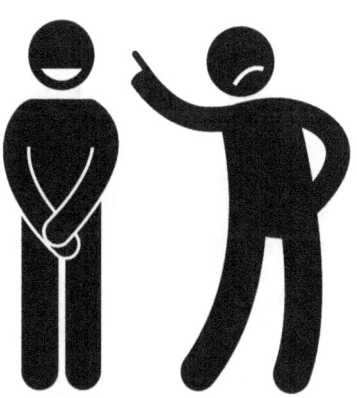

SES 31

A student's positive achievements are shared with other staff on a regular basis

Sharing student achievements with colleagues is important for several reasons. First, it helps to create a positive school culture. When students see that their achievements are being recognized, they feel valued and supported. This can lead to increased motivation and engagement in school. Second, sharing student achievements can help to build collegial relationships between teachers. When teachers see each other's students succeeding, it creates a sense of community and support. This can lead to increased collaboration and innovation in the classroom. Finally, sharing student achievements can help to raise the profile of the school. When parents and the community see that students are succeeding, they are more likely to support the school.

Here are a few ways you can promote student achievements into your learning environment routine:

Weekly Celebration Assemblies

This is a great way to recognize student achievements in front of a large audience. It can be as simple as having students come up to the front of the assembly and share their accomplishments. These are common in non-American schools.

All Share Staff Meetings

Take time at the beginning of each staff meeting to share positive reports about your students. This is a great way to start the week off on a positive note. It also gives teachers a chance to learn about what is going on in other classrooms.

Good News Monday

Weekly staff emails or shout-outs celebrating students. This is a quick and easy way to share student achievements with your colleagues. You can send out a weekly email or post a shout-out on social media.

REFLECTION: SOCIAL-EMOTIONAL STRENGTHENING

Take a few minutes to review the 30 C&I Key Strengths for neurodiversity and inclusion, and answer the following questions:

Which 3 Key Indicator(s) were you most impacted by:
1. _____
2. _____
3. _____

How do you plan on capitalizing on this in your classroom?
_____
_____
_____
_____

Create a complete list for how you currently set up your learning environment for SES success, including how you support others who work with you.

_____	_____
_____	_____
_____	_____
_____	_____
_____	_____

How can you support others' development in the area of SES?
_____
_____
_____
_____

> Do what you can, where you are, with what you have.
> —Teddy Roosevelt

DEEP DIVE
EXECUTIVE FUNCTIONING

EXECUTIVE FUNCTIONING PATHWAYS

The Executive Functioning Pathway will take you on a journey toward recognizing the tools and strategies that students with EF differences require to be successful in the learning environment and in their community. Within this section, you will encounter a series of strength statements that serve as guiding principles for creating an environment that celebrates neurodiversity and fosters the growth of every student, regardless of their EF differences. By embracing these practices and applying them diligently to your routines, you will establish a learning environment that acknowledges and respects the EF tools and accommodations these students require to reach their potential.

EXECUTIVE FUNCTIONING (EF)

Executive function (EF) and self-regulation skills are the mental processes that enable us to plan, focus attention, remember instructions, and juggle multiple tasks successfully. The three main utilities of EF include:

Cognitive Flexibility- Cognitive flexibility is the ability to view a variety of situations through different perspectives. Individuals with cognitive flexibility are able to find success despite unexpected issues that arise. These students learn how to adjust to change, adapt their thinking about issues when new facts present themselves, and can improvise well when sudden changes take place.

Working Memory- Working memory is the ability to hold information in mind and to creatively reorganize it to create new information. This is not to be confused with short-term memory, which is the ability to follow through with an instruction or information in sequential order. While working memory can rely on short-term memory, it permits individuals to:

- relate different ideas to one another
- reflect on past ideas and connect it to future implementation
- remember questions as you give attention to ongoing dialogue
- make sense of new information and relate it to current events

Inhibition Control (including self-control)- Inhibitory control is one's ability to control responses or actions and limit impulsivity. Many young people, including those with attention differences, find it difficult to control or hold back behavior even if they know it is not constructive.

Executive Functioning (EF) Warm-up

Before you read through the EF Pathway, consider the following:

How do you support student development of the three major EF utilities discussed on the previous page?

1. _____
_____
2. _____
_____
3. _____
_____

What environmental barriers and "old way" of doing things still exist in your learning environment that may prevent students from demonstrating self-management/independent skills?

Barriers:
_____
_____

What students need:
_____
_____

What I can try to do:
_____
_____

What strategies do you champion in your routines to support EF in your environment?

EF 1

Given homework is displayed in the same location within a classroom
When considering systems and routines for neurodiverse learners, consistency is key. Consistency helps establish routines so students can develop positive learning habits.

One way to create consistency is to display homework or other assignments in the same location. This supports classroom organization by maintaining a centralized location where items are displayed. It also helps teachers consistently monitor projects that have been assigned and when they are due. In addition to consistency, and other benefits including accessibility and accountability. Students with executive function (EF) differences benefit from having this information accessible as it does not rely solely on verbal directions from the teacher. Instead, the information is reinforced both visually and through classroom systems, reinforcing accountability in healthy and well-structured learning environments.

THINK ABOUT IT. Do you...
Have a display that is easy for students to see and access homework?

Use clear and concise language when labeling the display?

Update the display regularly to reflect new assignments?

Encourage students to check the display regularly for upcoming assignments?

EF 2

Large tasks or assignments are given "mini-deadlines" as a task analysis and small steps of progress are celebrated or acknowledged

Students with EF differences often find planning large tasks or projects difficult. Outstanding neurodiverse and inclusive learning environments promote independence by teaching students how to plan out larger projects. One key way to do this is by creating mini-deadlines. Consider how these points could look in your environment.

Mini-deadlines are small, achievable goals that can be broken down from a larger project. They help students:
- Make large projects less daunting. When a project is broken into smaller steps, it is less overwhelming
- Increase motivation. Mini-deadlines provide students with clear markers and Strengths for achievement, improving motivation
- Allow for better planning. When students know they what they need to accomplish, they can better plan their time and resources.
- Create opportunities for course correction. Through regular progress monitoring, students can identify areas where they may need to adjust their plans.
- Reinforce positive behavior. When students meet mini-deadlines, they are rewarded with positive reinforcement, which can help to encourage them in and out of the classroom.

Mini-deadlines are simple and effective for supporting students' EF differences. Here are specific tips for creating these:
- Break down the larger project into smaller, more manageable steps
- Set realistic deadlines for each step
- Provide students with regular feedback and encouragement
- Celebrate student success along the way

EF 3

Routines are explicitly taught and practiced

This program has highlighted routines, systems, and practices that are consistent in highly effective learning environments. These can take time to establish and must be explicitly taught and practiced by all—including those in charge!

Routines benefit everyone and will:
- Increase efficiency. When students and teachers know what to expect, they can move through their day more smoothly and efficiently.
- Improve skill performance. By reducing the cognitive load of planning a task, routines can free up students' and teachers' brains to focus on the task at hand.
- Reduce stress. When students and teachers know what to expect, they can feel more in control and less stressed.

To establish and maintain effective routines, be clear, be flexible, and stay positive.

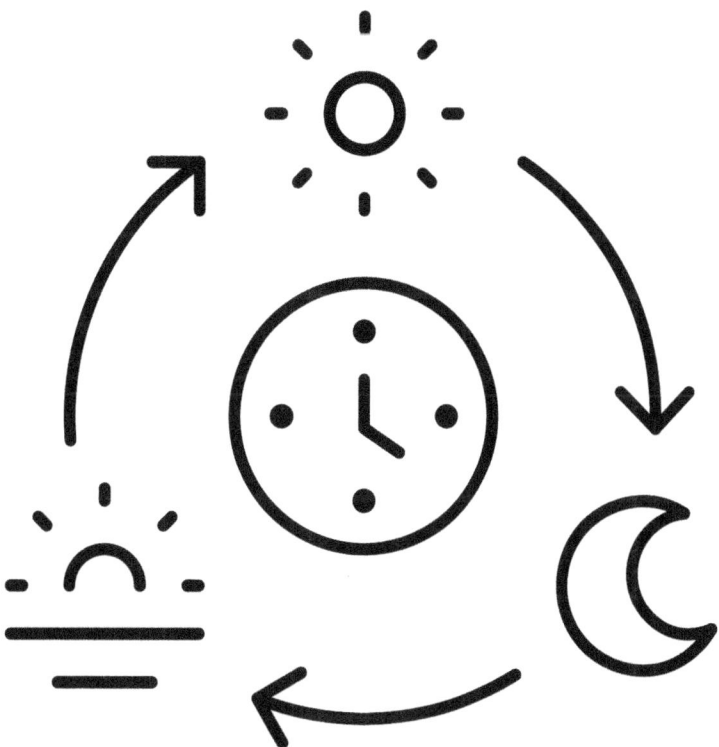

REFLECT & SHARE

Your daily routines (personal)

Your learning environment routines at the beginning of the day or lesson and at the end of day/lesson

Routines students know, follow, and take responsibility for

Any additional routines you think would help students organize develop greater autonomy

EF 4
Staff have grace for student mistakes and differences

"Grace" is an unmerited gift of kindness, or forgiveness. Teachers have plenty of opportunities to give grace to their students(!) and it requires wisdom to know when and how to give it. Having grace for students is important because:

- It promotes an inviting learning environment
- Mistakes are seen as opportunities for growth rather than punitive
- Giving grace builds relationships through communication and increased trust
- It models positive behavior by showing students how to interact with others with compassion and kindness

It is important to note that grace does not ignore issues, nor does it give permission to misbehave. It requires strength, consistency, and it upholds the highest standard.

REFLECT & SHARE
How have you experienced grace in your own life?

EF 5

The learning environment is free of clutter and unnecessary distractions

A clean learning environment demonstrates that a teacher respects the learning space, and it is essential for students. Clutter can be overwhelming and distracting, making it difficult to learn and focus. Neurodiverse learners who are educated in an environment free of clutter will have more respect for their classroom/space, which fosters a sense of safety, pride, and responsibility. Additionally, students will be able to focus better with fewer distractions. Ambitious educators can foster this by:

- Encouraging students to clean up to give them more ownership over the space
- Setting clear expectations for cleanliness and workspace standards
- Providing students with the tools and routines they need to declutter
- Being patient and offer students support if this is difficult for them

They say "Cleanliness is next to Godliness." They weren't wrong.

> **TAKE A MINUTE**
> **How can you de-clutter your learning spaces to help students maintain focus and organization?**

EF 6
Students are encouraged to work through their challenges and supported in doing so

Neurodiverse students who learn (and are taught) to work through their challenges in supportive learning environments possess a number of skills that will serve them well beyond school:

Greater confidence in their abilities and their support systems- Students who work through their challenges learn that they are capable of overcoming obstacles. They also learn that they have a network of people who can help them when needed.

Resilience for persevering through challenges in the learning environment and beyond- When students learn to work through their challenges, they develop resilience. This means they are able to bounce back from setbacks and continue to move forward.

Growth mindset helps them embrace challenges rather than shy away from them.

Independence to help them take ownership of their learning.

Increased engagement and motivation due to greater confidence in themselves and their network.

EF 7
Students use planners and organize tasks for the day and week

Planners help students stay organized by tracking assignments, due dates, and other vital information. Students who use these tend to manage and budget their time more effectively, which reduces stress and overwhelm. This helps them think through situations clearly and develop good study habits, which leads to better achievement.

When choosing planners, remember:
- Let students choose planners that work for them
- Be specific when writing assignments and due dates
- Teach students how to set realistic goals
- Set aside daily time to review planners
- Make changes if something isn't working (be flexible)

EF 8
Students use calendars to plan their week to reduce anxiety, strategize, and prioritize items

Neurodiverse learners who are learning to develop their executive functioning skills require support with planning activities and tasks throughout their day and week. This includes prioritizing, ordering, and learning together to create a roadmap to reach a goal (i.e., a task analysis). High quality learning environments support students' planning of activities through personalized calendars, timelines, daily planners, or datebooks and help students develop their own plans to complete multiple tasks. Doing so reduces anxiety, helps students strategize, and teaches them to prioritize events and tasks.

EF 9
Movement is incorporated into lesson routines

When students sit for long periods of time, they often become restless and lose focus. Movement can help avert this by keeping energy levels up, thus maintaining engagement in their learning. It can also improve retention of content, reduce stress, and increase creativity. Ambitious educators who build movement routines into their lessons avoid a number of pitfalls that can easily be avoided.

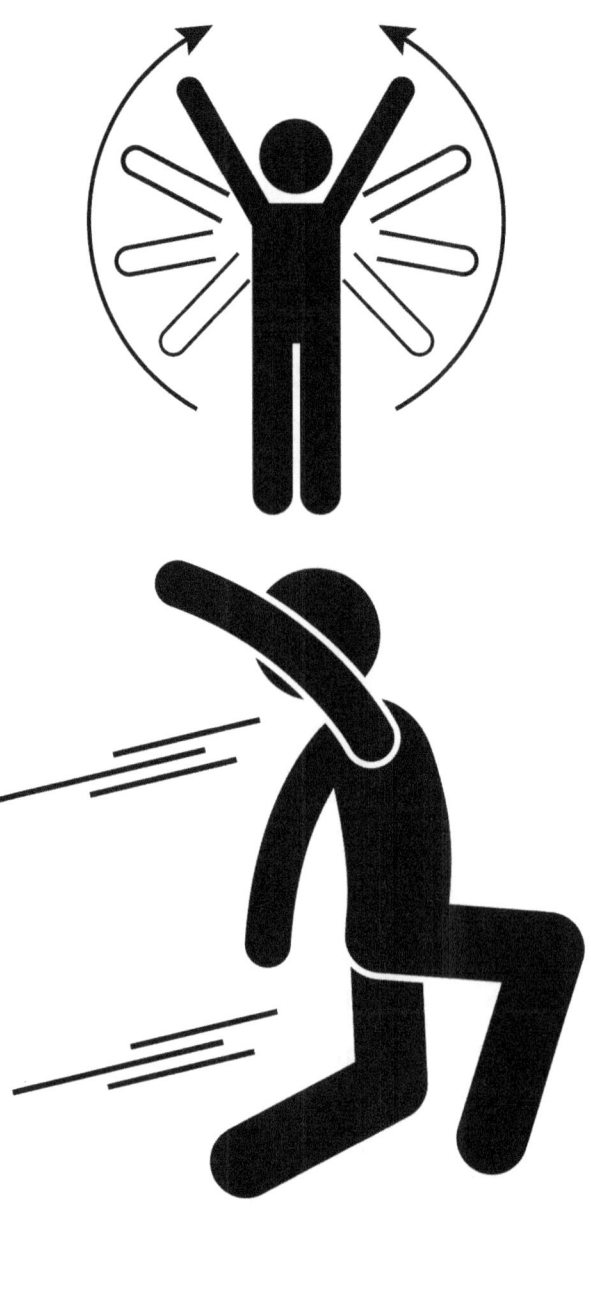

THINK ABOUT IT
In what ways do you incorporate movement into your routines?

EF 10
Students are encouraged to have grace for themselves

The adult anxiety epidemic has now unnecessarily reached children, and adults should tirelessly work to reverse this trend. From a young age, neurodiverse learners must be taught that it is okay to make mistakes. Mistakes provide opportunities for learning, resiliency, relationship-building, and if handled right – mental fortitude. When students are taught to have grace for themselves, they can laugh off their mistakes without judgment or condemnation, while being encouraged to engaged in self-reflection. This can foster more trusting relationships with peers and adults, and they will learn to treat themselves and others with kindness and compassion, maintaining a high standard.

THINK ABOUT IT
In what ways do you show grace for students?

EF 11
Staff can see when students are overwhelmed and quietly offer breaks, as needed

A number of factors can make it difficult for students to succeed. Students exhibiting EF differences often struggle to regulate their emotions, which can be particularly challenging in large group settings. While the ultimate goal is for these students to learn to thrive with their peers, their starting points may be very different. Ambitious educators who understand what these differences require, and help students navigate and take ownership over these challenges, establish supportive, trusting, and challenging opportunities for their neurodiverse learners to thrive.

REFLECT
How can you tell if your students are overwhelmed? What does it look like/sound like when they are overwhelmed?

Looks like:

Sounds like:

EF 12

Expectations for academic tasks are explicitly taught and displayed

Students with neurodiversities in the area of executive functioning often require support to develop:
- Planning and organization
- Task initiation
- Self-monitoring
- Task completion

These students require explicit instruction for a number of academic-based tasks. As already discussed extensively, rubrics are outstanding for mapping the skills required to successfully complete assignments. Students often require models and examples of expectations. Outstanding, ambitious teachers who understand this go out of their way to make this scaffold available for all students, and those who require it will use it. This is a difference – not a deficit – and it should be viewed as such!

> **REFLECT**
> **Who are these students and what do they need to succeed?**

EF 13
Time checks and countdowns are used during work periods to help students effectively budget their time

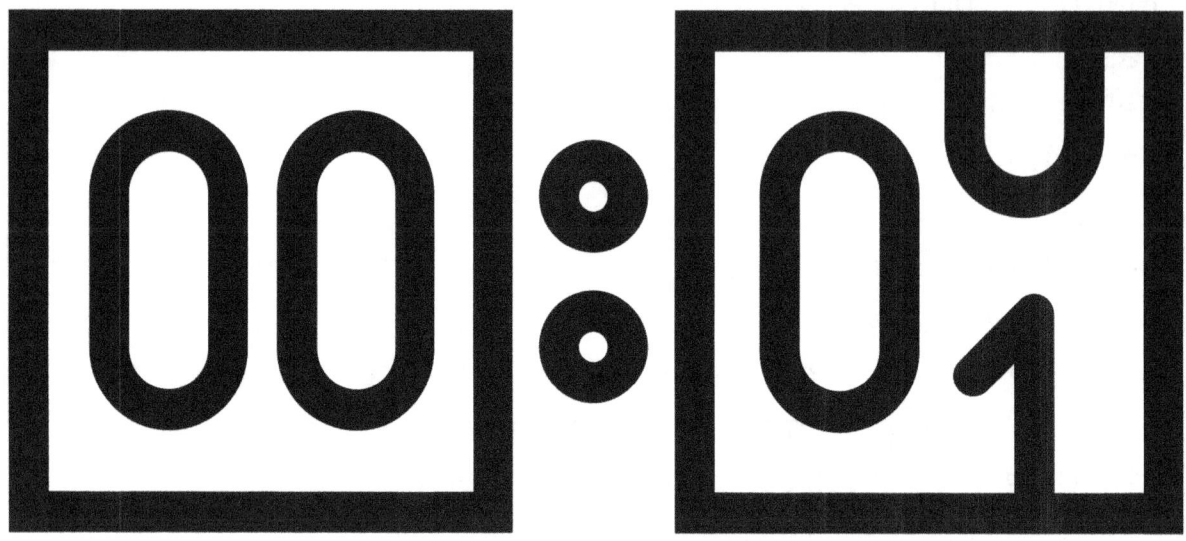

Learning environments that are supportive of EF differences help students manage and budget lesson time effectively. This can take the form of countdown clocks (digital or analog) or timers, time management task planners at a student's desk (e.g., spend 5-minutes on __, 12 minutes on __), or other planning resources discussed that help students learn how to manage their time. This can help them prioritize their work, stay engaged and avoid distractions for short periods of time which will help them become more productive, efficient, and successful in school and beyond!

EF 14
Students have access to checklists for items needed in an assignment or project

Checklists provide a visual task analysis of items that need to be completed, which helps students break down numerous larger tasks into smaller, more manageable steps. This can reduce overwhelm and increase motivation, as students can see progress being made when they complete each item. Checklists, as discussed throughout this program, also develop a sense of personal responsibility and a clear record of accountability for neurodiverse learners. This allows students to take ownership over their learning and educational experiences, thus helping them develop independence. Finally, checklists reduce the cognitive load required to remember the tasks a student must complete. By creating a written record of the tasks necessary and referring to these, students no longer have to retain (memorize) information, which frees up working memory and mental capacity. This simple yet effective tool helps neurodiverse learners stay organized and manage their time effectively, in order to achieve their goals.

Use some of the templates here as you see fit!

To Do

- [ ] _____
- [ ] _____
- [ ] _____
- [ ] _____

CHECKLIST

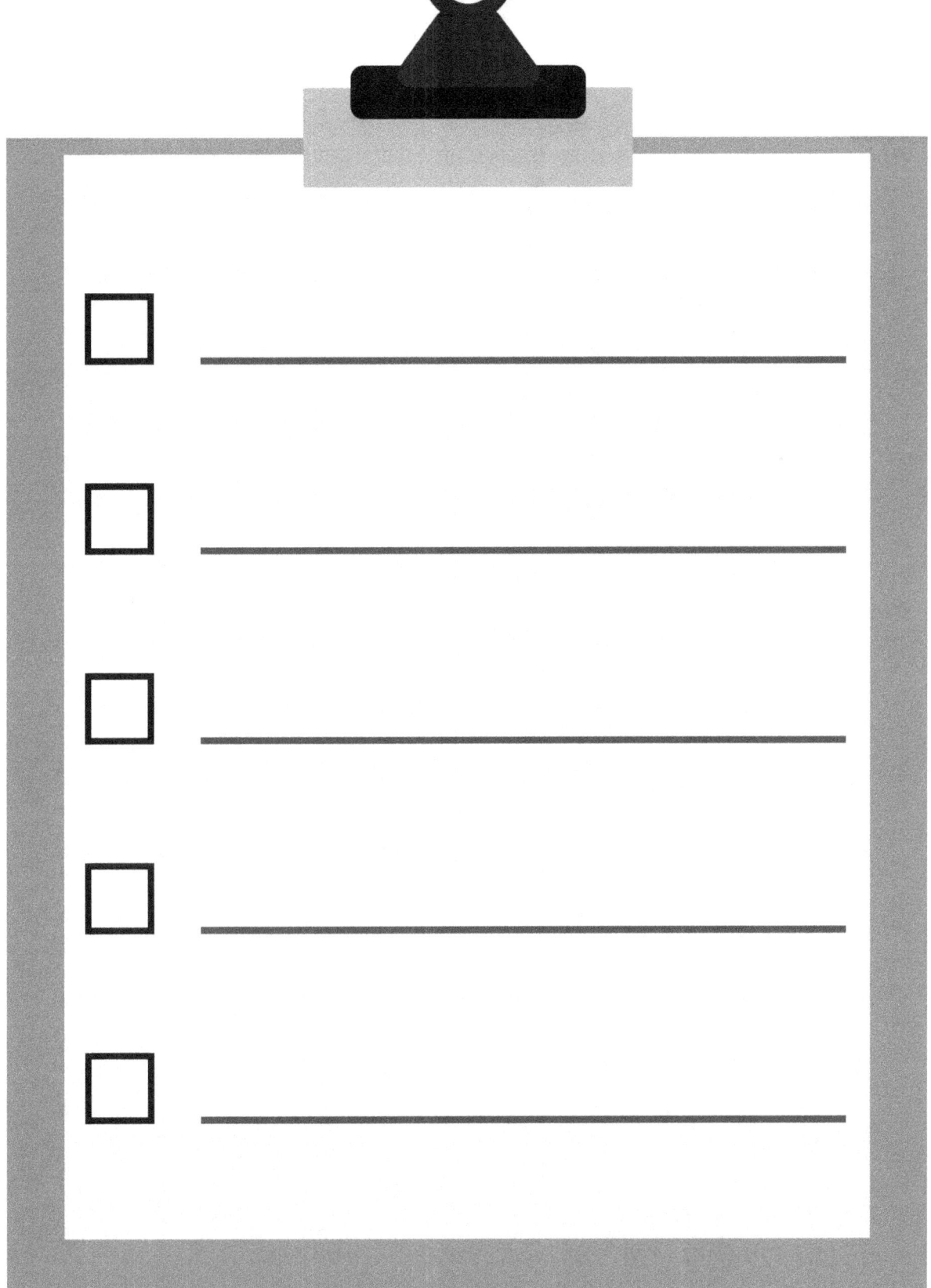

EF 15
Glossy materials are avoided to eliminate visual stress
Glossy books and resources create glare and reflections that creates unnecessary distraction and hinder reading comprehension. This can ultimately lead to problematic and off-task behaviors. When light reflects off a screen or a page, learners spend time trying to eliminate the glare by moving around, regularly rotating the object, or they might even try to push through it. Unfortunately, this rarely yields success. To reduce this stress, use non-reflective surfaces or materials wherever possible, especially when students are required to spend extended time looking at these resources.

REFLECTION: EXECUTIVE FUNCTIONING

Take a few minutes to review the 15 EF Key Strengths for neurodiversity and inclusion, and answer the following questions:

Which 3 EF Strengths were you most impacted by:
1. _____
2. _____
3. _____

How do you plan on adding more of these to your environment's daily routines or practices?
_____
_____
_____
_____

Create a complete list for how you currently set up your learning environment for EF success, including how you support others who work with you.

_____	_____
_____	_____
_____	_____
_____	_____
_____	_____
_____	_____

How will you support others' EF strength development?
_____
_____
_____
_____

> If you can dream it, you can do it
> -Walt Disney

Part 3
Research Supporting The Four Key Strengths of High Quality Learning Environments

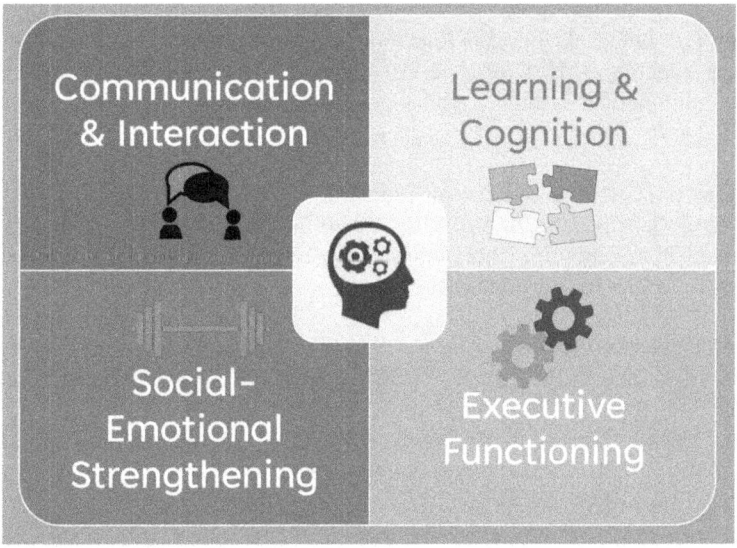

> The most difficult thing is the decision to act, the rest is merely tenacity.
> –Amelia Earhart

BIBLIOGRAPHY

COMMUNICATION & INTERACTION

C&I 1-
Marzano, R. J., Marzano, J. S., & Pickering, D. J. (2003). Classroom management that works: Research-based strategies for every teacher. ASCD.

C&I 2-
Jones, F. H., & Jones, P. S. (2019). Tools for Teaching: Discipline, Instruction, Motivation. Fredric H. Jones & Associates, Inc.

C&I 3-
Fisher, D., & Frey, N. (2014). Better learning through structured teaching: A framework for the gradual release of responsibility. Alexandria, VA: ASCD.
Marzano, R. J., & Simms, J.A. (2013). Vocabulary for the common core. Bloomington, IN: Marzano Research Laboratory.

C&I 4-
Cook SW, Duffy RG, Fenn KM. Consolidation and transfer of learning after observing hand gesture. Child Dev. 2013 Nov-Dec;84(6):1863-71. doi: 10.1111/cdev.12097. Epub 2013 Mar 28. PMID: 23551027.
Goldin-Meadow S, Cook SW, Mitchell ZA. Gesturing gives children new ideas about math. Psychol Sci. 2009 Mar;20(3):267-72. doi: 10.1111/j.1467-9280.2009.02297.x. Epub 2009 Feb 13. PMID: 19222810; PMCID: PMC2750886.

C&I 5-
Mayer, R. E. (2009). Multimedia Learning. Cambridge: Cambridge University Press. https://doi.org/10.1017/CBO9780511811678

C&I 6-
Fiorella, L., & Mayer, R. E. (2016). Eight ways to promote generative learning. Educational Psychology Review, 28(4), 717–741. https://doi.org/10.1007/s10648-015-9348-9
Mayer, R. E. (2001). Multimedia Learning. Cambridge University Press.
Paivio, A. (1971). Imagery and verbal processes. Holt, Rinehart & Winston.

C&I 7-
Rosenshine, B., & Meister, C. (1994). Reciprocal Teaching: A Review of the Research. Review of Educational Research, 64(4), 479–530. https://doi.org/10.3102/00346543064004479
Sweller, J. (1988). Cognitive load during problem solving: Effects on learning. Cognitive Science, 12(2), 257–285. https://doi.org/10.1207/s15516709cog1202_4

C&I 8-
Quill KA. Instructional considerations for young children with autism: the rationale for visually cued instruction. J Autism Dev Disord. 1997 Dec;27(6):697-714. doi: 10.1023/a:1025806900162. PMID: 9455729.

C&I 9-
Mayer, R. E. (2014). Cognitive theory of multimedia learning. In R. E. Mayer (Ed.), The Cambridge handbook of multimedia learning (pp. 43–71). Cambridge University Press. https://doi.org/10.1017/CBO9781139547369.005

C&I 10-
Fiorella, L., & Mayer, R. (2015). *Learning as a Generative Activity: Eight Learning Strategies that Promote Understanding*. Cambridge: Cambridge University Press. doi:10.1017/CBO9781107707085

C&I 11-
Darling-Hammond L, Adamson F. Beyond Basic Skills: The Role of Performance Assessment in Achieving 21st Century Standards of Learning. Stanford Center for Opportunity Policy in Education. 2012.
Wiggins, Grant P. Educative assessment: Designing assessments to inform and improve student performance. Vol. 1. San Francisco, CA: Jossey-Bass, 1998.

C&I 12-
Mayer, R. E. (2014). Cognitive theory of multimedia learning. In R. E. Mayer (Ed.), The Cambridge handbook of multimedia learning (pp. 43–71). Cambridge University Press. https://doi.org/10.1017/CBO9781139547369.005
Sweller J; Ayres PL; Kalyuga S, 2011, Cognitive load theory, Explorations in the Learning Sciences Instructional Systems, Springer, New York, http://dx.doi.org/10.1007/978-1-4419-8126-4

C&I 13-
Rowe, M. B., "Wait-time and rewards as instructional variables, their influence on language, logic, and fate control: part one-wait-time," Journal of Research in Science Teaching, vol. 11, no. 4, pp. 81-94, 1974.

C&I 14-
Rosenshine, B.V. (2012). Principles of Instruction: Research-Based Strategies That All Teachers Should Know. *The American Educator, 36*, 12.

C&I 15-
Kalyuga, S., Chandler, P., & Sweller, J. (1999). Managing split-attention and redundancy in multimedia instruction. Applied Cognitive Psychology, 13(4), 351–371. https://doi.org/10.1002/(SICI)1099-0720(199908)13:4<351::AID-ACP589>3.0.CO;2-6
Mayer, R. E., & Moreno, R. (2003). Nine ways to reduce cognitive load in multimedia learning. Educational psychologist, 38(1), 43-52

C&I 16-
Dunlosky, J., Rawson, K. A., Marsh, E. J., Nathan, M. J., & Willingham, D. T. (2013). Improving students' learning with effective learning techniques: Promising directions from cognitive and educational psychology. Psychological Science in the Public Interest, 14(1), 4-58.
Roediger, H. L. III, & Butler, A. C. (2011). The critical role of retrieval practice in long-term retention. Trends in Cognitive Sciences, 15(1), 20–27. https://doi.org/10.1016/j.tics.2010.09.003

C&I 17-
Archibald, L. M. (2017). SLP-educator classroom collaboration: A review to inform reason-based practice. Autism & Developmental Language Impairments, 2. https://doi.org/10.1177/2396941516680369
Gallagher AL, Murphy CA, Conway PF, Perry A. Engaging multiple stakeholders to improve speech and language therapy services in schools: an appreciative inquiry-based study. BMC Health Serv Res. 2019 Apr 15;19(1):226. doi: 10.1186/s12913-019-4051-z. PMID: 30987610; PMCID: PMC6466713.
Justice, L. M., & Pullen, P. C. (2003). Promising Interventions for Promoting Emergent Literacy Skills: Three Evidence-Based Approaches. Topics in Early Childhood Special Education, 23(3), 99–113. https://doi.org/10.1177/02711214030230030101
Law J, Dennis JA, Charlton JJV. Speech and language therapy interventions for children with primary speech and/or language disorders. Cochrane Database Syst Rev. 2017 Jan 9;2017(1):CD012490. doi: 10.1002/14651858.CD012490. PMCID: PMC6464758.

LEARNING & COGNITION
L&C 1-
Berninger VW, Nielsen KH, Abbott RD, Wijsman E, Raskind W. Writing problems in developmental dyslexia: under-recognized and under-treated. J Sch Psychol. 2008 Feb;46(1):1-21. doi: 10.1016/j.jsp.2006.11.008. PMID: 18438452; PMCID: PMC2344144.
Miller AC, Keenan JM, Betjemann RS, Willcutt EG, Pennington BF, Olson RK. Reading comprehension in children with ADHD: cognitive underpinnings of the centrality deficit. J Abnorm Child Psychol. 2013 Apr;41(3):473-83. doi: 10.1007/s10802-012-9686-8. PMID: 23054132; PMCID: PMC3561476.
Poll GH, Miller CA, Mainela-Arnold E, Adams KD, Misra M, Park JS. Effects of children's working memory capacity and processing speed on their sentence imitation performance. Int J Lang Commun Disord. 2013 May-Jun;48(3):329-42. doi: 10.1111/1460-6984.12014. Epub 2013 Mar 25. PMID: 23650889.

L&C 2-
Beck, I. L., McKeown, M. G., & Kucan, L. (2008). Bringing Words to Life: Robust Vocabulary Instruction. Guilford Press.
Jitendra, A. K., Edwards, L. L., Sacks, G., & Jacobson, L. A. (2004). What research says about vocabulary instruction for students with learning disabilities. Exceptional children, 70(3), 299-322. https://doi.org/10.1177/001440290407000303
Marzano, Robert J. (2004). Building background knowledge for academic achievement : research on what works in schools. Alexandria, VA :Association for Supervision and Curriculum Development,

L&C 4-
Ausubel, D. P. (1960). The use of advance organizers in the learning and retention of meaningful verbal material. Journal of Educational Psychology, 51, 267-272. http://dx.doi.org/10.1037/h0046669
Mayer, R. E. (2003). The promise of multimedia learning: Using the same instructional design methods across different media. Learning and Instruction, 13(2), 125–139. https://doi.org/10.1016/S0959-4752(02)00016-6
National Research Council. 2000. How People Learn: Brain, Mind, Experience, and School: Expanded Edition. Washington, DC: The National Academies Press. https://doi.org/10.17226/9853.

L&C 5-
Balagopal, S., & Young, P. (Dec. 2001/Jan. 2002). Increasing independence in inclusive settings. Closing the Gap, 20(5), 1-16.
Dalton, B. D., Herbert, M., & Deysher, S. (2003). Scaffolding students' response to digital literature with embedded strategy supports: The role of audio-recording vs. writing student response options. 53rd Annual Meeting of the National Reading Conference.
Darling-Hammond, Linda & Bransford, John & Lepage, Pamela & Hammerness, Karen & Duffy, Helen. (2005). Preparing Teachers for a Changing World: What teachers should learn and be able to do.

Quenneville, J. (2001). Tech tools for students with learning disabilities: Infusion into inclusive classrooms.Preventing School Failure, 45(4), 167-170.

L&C 6-

Agarwal, P. K., Bain, P. M., & Chamberlain, R. W. (2012). The Value of Applied Research: Retrieval Practice Improves Classroom Learning and Recommendations From a Teacher, a Principal, and a Scientist. Educational Psychology Review, 24(3), 437-448.

Dunlosky, J., Rawson, K. A., Marsh, E. J., Nathan, M. J., & Willingham, D. T. (2013). Improving Students' Learning With Effective Learning Techniques: Promising Directions From Cognitive and Educational Psychology. Psychological Science in the Public Interest, 14(1), 4-58.

Marzano, R. J., Pickering, D. J., & Pollock, J. E. (2001). Classroom Instruction That Works: Research-Based Strategies for Increasing Student Achievement. ASCD

L&C 7-

Black, P., & Wiliam, D. (2010). Inside the Black Box: Raising Standards through Classroom Assessment. Phi Delta Kappan, 92(1), 81–90. https://doi.org/10.1177/003172171009200119

Frey N. Hattie J. & Fisher D. (2018). Developing assessment-capable visible learners grades k-12 : maximizing skill will and thrill (First). Corwin Literacy.

Shepard, L. A. (2000). The Role of Assessment in a Learning Culture. Educational Researcher, 29(7), 4–14. https://doi.org/10.3102/0013189X029007004

L&C 8-

Hattie, J. (2009). Visible Learning: A synthesis of over 800 meta-analyses relating to achievement. Routledge.

Mayer, R. E., & Moreno, R. (2003). Nine ways to reduce cognitive load in multimedia learning. Educational Psychologist, 38(1), 43-52.

Paivio, A. (1971). Imagery and verbal processes. Holt, Rinehart & Winston.

L&C 9-

Graham, S., and Hebert, M.. *Writing to Read: Evidence for How Writing Can Improve. Carnegie Corporation Time to Act Report.* Washington, DC: Alliance for Excellent Education, 2010. Print.

Graham, S.; Perin, D., Writing Next: Effective Strategies to Improve Writing of Adolescents in Middle and High Schools

Scardamalia, M., & Bereiter, C. (1987). Knowledge Telling and Knowledge Transforming in Written Composition. In S. Rosenberg (Eds.), Advances in Applied Psycholinguistics, Volume 2: Reading, Writing and Language Learning (pp. 142-175). Cambridge University Press.

L&C 10-

Hattie, J. (2012). Visible learning for teachers: Maximizing impact on learning. Routledge/Taylor & Francis Group. https://doi.org/10.4324/9780203181522

Marzano, R. J. (2004). Building background knowledge for academic achievement: Research on what works in schools. ASCD.

Mayer, R. E., & Sims, V. K. (1994). For whom is a picture worth a thousand words? Extensions of a dual-coding theory of multimedia learning. Journal of Educational Psychology, 86(3), 389-401.

L&C 11-

Black, P., & Wiliam, D. (1998). Inside the Black Box: Raising Standards Through Classroom Assessment. Phi Delta Kappan, 80(2), 139-148.

Coker, D. L., & Ritchey, K. D. (2010). Curriculum-Based Measurement of Writing in Kindergarten and First Grade: An Investigation of Production and Qualitative Scores. Exceptional Children, 76(2), 175–193. https://doi.org/10.1177/001440291007600203

Graham, S., & Perin, D. (2007). Writing Next: Effective Strategies to Improve Writing of Adolescents in Middle and High Schools. Alliance for Excellent Education.

Sadler, D. R. (1983). Evaluation and the improvement of learning. Journal of Higher Education, 54(1), 60-79.

L&C 12-

Andrade, H. G. (2000). Using rubrics to promote thinking and learning. Educational Leadership, 57(5), 13-18.

Black, P., & Wiliam, D. (1998). Inside the Black Box: Raising Standards Through Classroom Assessment. Phi Delta Kappan, 80(2), 139-148.

Coker, D. L., & Ritchey, K. D. (2010). Curriculum-Based Measurement of Writing in Kindergarten and First Grade: An Investigation of Production and Qualitative Scores. Exceptional Children, 76(2), 175–193. https://doi.org/10.1177/001440291007600203

L&C 14-

Mayer, R. E. (2014). Cognitive theory of multimedia learning. The Cambridge Handbook of Multimedia Learning, 43-71.

Mayer, R. E., & Moreno, R. (2003). Nine ways to reduce cognitive load in multimedia learning. Educational Psychologist, 38(1), 43-52.

L&C 15-
Pile, E. A., & Devereux, E. (2016). The Effect of Coloured Paper on Readability of Written Text: Evidence from Dyslexic and Non-Dyslexic Readers. Dyslexia, 22(3), 238-245.
Wilkins, A. J., Lewis, E., Smith, F., & Rowland, E. (2001). Coloured Overlays and Their Benefit for Reading. Journal of Research in Reading, 24(2), 129-143.

L&C 16-
Allington, R. L. (2012). What Really Matters for Struggling Readers: Designing Research-Based Programs. Pearson Allyn Bacon Prentice Hall.

L&C 17-
Allington, R. L. (2012). What Really Matters for Struggling Readers: Designing Research-Based Programs. Pearson Allyn Bacon Prentice Hall.

L&C 18-
Mayer, R. E., & Moreno, R. (2003). Nine ways to reduce cognitive load in multimedia learning. Educational Psychologist, 38(1), 43-52.
Plass, J.L., Homer, B.D. & Hayward, E.O. Design factors for educationally effective animations and simulations. J Comput High Educ 21, 31–61 (2009). https://doi.org/10.1007/s12528-009-9011-x
Sweller, J. (2006). The worked example effect and human cognition. Learning and Instruction, 16(2), 165-169.

L&C 19-
Legge GE, Bigelow CA. Does print size matter for reading? A review of findings from vision science and typography. J Vis. 2011 Aug 9;11(5):10.1167/11.5.8 8. doi: 10.1167/11.5.8. PMID: 21828237; PMCID: PMC3428264.
Phillips, D.J.P., (2014). How to avoid death by PowerPoint. Ted.X Stockholm. YouTube. https://www.youtube.com/watch?v=Iwpi1Lm6dFo
Roorda, A., Williams, D. The arrangement of the three cone classes in the living human eye. Nature 397, 520–522 (1999). https://doi.org/10.1038/17383

L&C 20-
Mayer, R. E. (2009). Multimedia Learning: Second Edition. Cambridge University Press.

L&C 21-
Deshler, D. D., Ellis, E. S., & Lenz, B. K. (1996). Teaching adolescents with learning disabilities: Strategies and methods. Allyn & Bacon.
Elliott, S. N., Kratochwill, T. R., & Cook, J. L. (1999). Educational psychology: Effective teaching, effective learning. McGraw-Hill.
Graham, S., Harris, K. R., & Mason, L. (2005). Improving the writing performance, knowledge, and self efficacy of struggling young writers: The effects of self-regulated strategy development. Contemporary Educational Psychology, 30(2), 207-241.

L&C 22-
Dunlosky, J., Rawson, K. A., Marsh, E. J., Nathan, M. J., & Willingham, D. T. (2013). Improving students' learning with effective learning techniques: Promising directions from cognitive and educational psychology. Psychological Science in the Public Interest, 14(1), 4–58. https://doi.org/10.1177/1529100612453266

L&C 23-
Kalyuga, S., Chandler, P., & Sweller, J. (2000). Incorporating learner experience into the design of multimedia instruction. Journal of Educational Psychology, 92(1), 126–136. https://doi.org/10.1037/0022-0663.92.1.126
Mayer, R. E., & Johnson, C. I. (2008). Revising the redundancy principle in multimedia learning. Journal of Educational Psychology, 100(2), 380–386. https://doi.org/10.1037/0022-0663.100.2.380
Tindall-Ford, S., Chandler, P., & Sweller, J. (1997). When two sensory modes are better than one. Journal of Experimental Psychology: Applied, 3(4), 257–287. https://doi.org/10.1037/1076-898X.3.4.257

L&C 24-
Chi, M. T. H., Bassok, M., Lewis, M. W., Reimann, P., & Glaser, R. (1989). Self-explanations: How students study and use examples in learning to solve problems. Cognitive Science, 13(2), 145-182.
Rosenshine, B. (2012) Principles of Instruction: Research-Based Strategies That All Teachers Should Know. American Educator, 36(1), p12-39.

L&C 25-
Hattie, J., & Timperley, H. (2007). The Power of Feedback. Review of Educational Research, 77(1), 81–112. https://doi.org/10.3102/003465430298487
Nicol, D., & Macfarlane, D. (2006). Formative Assessment and Self-Regulated Learning: A Model and Seven Principles of Good Feedback Practice. Studies in Higher Education. 31. 199-218. 10.1080/03075070600572090.
Shute, V. J. (2008). Focus on Formative Feedback. Review of Educational Research, 78(1), 153–189. https://doi.org/10.3102/0034654307313795

L&C 26-
Mercer, N., & Littleton, K., (2007). Dialogue and the development of children's thinking: a sociocultural approach. London, UK: Routledge.
Slavin, R.E. (2015). Cooperative learning in elementary schools. Education 3-13, 43(1), 5-14.
Webb, N. M. (2009). The teacher's role in promoting collaborative dialogue in the classroom. British Journal of Educational Psychology, 79(1), 1–28. https://doi.org/10.1348/000709908X380772

L&C 27-
Desforges, C. & Abouchaar, A. (2003) The impact of parental involvement, parental support and family education on pupil achievement and adjustment: A literature review. London: Department for Education and Skills.
Epstein, J.L. (2011). School, Family, and Community Partnerships: Preparing Educators and Improving Schools (2nd ed.). Routledge. https://doi.org/10.4324/9780429494673
Fan, X., & Chen, M. (2001). Parental involvement and students' academic achievement: A meta-analysis. Educational Psychology Review, 13(1), 1–22. https://doi.org/10.1023/A:1009048817385

L&C 28-
Dunlosky, J., Rawson, K. A., Marsh, E. J., Nathan, M. J., & Willingham, D. T. (2013). Improving students' learning with effective learning techniques: Promising directions from cognitive and educational psychology. Psychological Science in the Public Interest, 14(1), 4-58.
Flavell, J. H. (1979). Metacognition and cognitive monitoring: A new area of cognitive–developmental inquiry. American Psychologist, 34(10), 906–911. https://doi.org/10.1037/0003-066X.34.10.906
Zimmerman, B. J. (2002). Becoming a Self-Regulated Learner: An Overview. Theory into Practice, 41, 64-70. http://dx.doi.org/10.1207/s15430421tip4102_2

SOCIAL-EMOTIONAL STRENGTHENING

SES 1-
Dweck, C. S. (2000). Self-theories: Their role in motivation, personality, and development. Psychology Press.

SES 2-
Blackwell, L. S., Trzesniewski, K. H., & Dweck, C. S. (2007). Implicit theories of intelligence predict achievement across an adolescent transition: A longitudinal study and an intervention. Child Development, 78(1), 246-263.
Mueller, C. M., & Dweck, C. S. (1998). Praise for intelligence can undermine children's motivation and performance. Journal of Personality and Social Psychology, 75(1), 33-52.
Yeager, D. S., Dweck, C. S., & Walton, G. M. (2013). Social-psychological interventions in education: They're not magic. Review of Educational Research, 83(4), 471-512.

SES 3-
Hattie, J. (2012). Visible learning for teachers: Maximizing impact on learning. Routledge/Taylor & Francis Group. https://doi.org/10.4324/9780203181522
Johnson, D. W., & Johnson, R. T. (2009). An Educational Psychology Success Story: Social Interdependence Theory and Cooperative Learning. Educational Researcher, 38(5), 365–379. https://doi.org/10.3102/0013189X09339057
Slavin, R.E. (2015). Cooperative learning in elementary schools. Education 3-13, 43(1), 5-14.

SES 5-
Honey, M. (Ed.). (2013). Design, Make, Play: Growing the Next Generation of STEM Innovators (1st ed.). Routledge. https://doi.org/10.4324/9780203108352
Kolb, D. A. (2014). Experiential Learning: Experience as the Source of Learning and Development. New Jersey: FT Press.

SES 7-
Jennings, P. A., & Greenberg, M. T. (2009). The prosocial classroom: Teacher social and emotional competence in relation to student and classroom outcomes. Review of Educational Research, 79(1), 491–525. https://doi.org/10.3102/0034654308325693
Rimm-Kaufman, S. E., Pianta, R. C., & Cox, M. J. (2000). Teachers' judgments of problems in the transition to kindergarten. Early Childhood Research Quarterly, 15(2), 147–166. https://doi.org/10.1016/S0885-2006(00)00049-1
Taylor RD, Oberle E, Durlak JA, Weissberg RP. Promoting Positive Youth Development Through School-Based Social and Emotional Learning Interventions: A Meta-Analysis of Follow-Up Effects. Child Dev. 2017 Jul;88(4):1156-1171. doi: 10.1111/cdev.12864. PMID: 28685826.

SES 8-
The Gallup Organization. (2006). The Clifton Youth StrengthsExplorer Assessment: Identifying the Talents of Today's Youth. Gallup Press

Seligman, M. E. P., Steen, T. A., Park, N., & Peterson, C. (2005). Positive Psychology Progress: Empirical Validation of Interventions. American Psychologist, 60(5), 410–421. Waters, L. E. (2015). Strength-based parenting and life satisfaction in teenagers. Advances in Social Sciences Research Journal, 2(11). https://doi.org/10.14738/assrj.211.1651

SES 9-
Brazeau, J.N., Teatero, M.L., Rawana, E.P. et al. The Strengths Assessment Inventory: Reliability of a New Measure of Psychosocial Strengths for Youth. J Child Fam Stud 21, 384–390 (2012). https://doi.org/10.1007/s10826-011-9489-5

Durlak J.A., Weissberg R..P, Dymnicki A.B., Taylor R..D, Schellinger K..B. The impact of enhancing students' social and emotional learning: a meta-analysis of school-based universal interventions. Child Dev. 2011 Jan-Feb;82(1):405-32. doi: 10.1111/j.1467-8624.2010.01564.x. PMID: 21291449.

Peterson, C., & Seligman, M. E. P. (2004). Character strengths and virtues: A handbook and classification. Washington, DC: American Psychological Association; New York: Oxford University Press.

SES 10-
Jennings, P. A., & Greenberg, M. T. (2009). The prosocial classroom: Teacher social and emotional competence in relation to student and classroom outcomes. Review of Educational Research, 79(1), 491–525. https://doi.org/10.3102/0034654308325693

Roffey, Sue. (2013). Inclusive and exclusive belonging -the impact on individual and community well-being. Educational and Child Psychology. 30. 38-49. 10.53841/bpsecp.2013.30.1.38.

SES 11-
Simonsen, Brandi & Falcon, Sarah & Briesch, Amy & Myers, Diane & Sugai, George. (2008). Evidence-based Practices in Classroom Management: Considerations for Research to Practice. Education and Treatment of Children. 31. 351-380. 10.1353/etc.0.0007.

SES 12-
Dweck, C. S. (2006). Mindset: The New Psychology of Success. New York: Random House Publishing Group.
Skinner, E. A., Furrer, C., Marchand, G., & Kindermann, T. (2008). Engagement and disaffection in the classroom: Part of a larger motivational dynamic? Journal of Educational Psychology, 100(4), 765-781.

SES 13-
Ahmed W, Minnaert A, van der Werf G, Kuyper H. Perceived social support and early adolescents' achievement: the mediational roles of motivational beliefs and emotions. J Youth Adolesc. 2010 Jan;39(1):36-46. doi: 10.1007/s10964-008-9367-7. Epub 2008 Nov 20. PMID: 20091215; PMCID: PMC2796962.

SES 14-
Gable, R. A., Hester, P. H., Rock, M. L., & Hughes, K. G. (2009). Back to basics: Rules, praise, ignoring and reprimands revisited. Intervention in Schools and Clinics, 44, 195-205

SES 15-
Lane, K. L., Wehby, J., Menzies, H. M., Doukas, G. L., Munton, S. M., & Gregg, R. M. (2003). Social skills instruction for students at risk for antisocial behavior: The effects of small-group instruction. Behavioral Disorders, 28(3), 229–248.

Mitchell, B. S., Kern, L., & Conroy, M. A. (2019). Supporting Students With Emotional or Behavioral Disorders: State of the Field. Behavioral Disorders, 44(2), 70–84. https://doi.org/10.1177/0198742918816518

Sugai, George & Horner, Robert. (2006). A Promising Approach for Expanding and Sustaining School-Wide Positive Behavior Support. School Psychology Review. 35. 10.1080/02796015.2006.12087989.

SES 16-
Watkins, C. (2011). Learning: a sense-maker's guide. London: Association of Teachers and Lecturers

SES 17-
Offering students independent access to multi-sensory resources, stress-relieving tools, and transition objects aligns with inclusive education, self-regulation support, and promoting smooth transitions. These resources empower students to regulate their sensory experiences, emotions, and transitions, ultimately enhancing their engagement, well-being, and learning outcomes.

SES 18-
Hattie, J. (2008). Visible Learning: A Synthesis of Over 800 Meta-Analyses Relating to Achievement (1st ed.). Routledge. https://doi.org/10.4324/9780203887332

Mayer, R. E. (2001). Multimedia learning. Cambridge University Press.

Prince, M. (2004). Does active learning work? A review of the research. Journal of Engineering Education, 93(3), 223-231.

SES 19-
Setting explicit, achievable behavior expectations through student targets, explanations, and modeling aligns with proactive behavior support, effective discipline, and successful interventions. These strategies create a positive learning environment and support students' understanding and adherence to behavioral norms.

SES 20-
Hattie, J., & TimpGerley, H. (2007). The Power of Feedback. Review of Educational Research, 77(1), 81–112. https://doi.org/10.3102/003465430298487
Kluger, A. N., & DeNisi, A. (1996). The effects of feedback interventions on performance: A historical review, a meta-analysis, and a preliminary feedback intervention theory. Psychological Bulletin, 119(2), 254–284. https://doi.org/10.1037/0033-2909.119.2.254

SES 21-
Roeser RW, Peck SC. An Education in Awareness: Self, Motivation, and Self-Regulated Learning in Contemplative Perspective. Educ Psychol. 2009 Apr 1;44(2):119-136. doi: 10.1080/00461520902832376. PMID: 20419040; PMCID: PMC2858411.

SES 22-
Hidi, S., & Renninger, K. A. (2006). The Four-Phase Model of Interest Development. Educational Psychologist, 41(2), 111–127. https://doi.org/10.1207/s15326985ep4102_4
Vygotsky, L. S. (1978). Mind in society: The development of higher psychological processes. Harvard University Press.

SES 23-
Evertson, C. M., & Emmer, E. T. (2017). Classroom management for elementary teachers (10th ed.). New York: Pearson. from The IRIS Center. (2002, 2012, 2021). Classroom behavior management (Part 2, Elementary): Developing a behavior management plan. Retrieved from https://iris.peabody.vanderbilt.edu/module/beh2_elem/
Gable, R. A., Hester, P. H., Rock, M. L., & Hughes, K. G. (2009). Back to basics: Rules, praise, ignoring and reprimands revisited. Intervention in Schools and Clinics, 44, 195-205

SES 24-
Such communication promotes a sense of dignity, trust, and mutual respect, enhancing students' engagement and overall well-being.

SES 25-
These discussions enable students to take ownership of their actions, reflect on their behavior, and work collaboratively towards positive conduct and learning experiences.

SES 26-
Roeser, Robert & Eccles, Jacquelynne & Sameroff, Arnold. (2000). School as a Context of Early Adolescents' Academic and Social-Emotional Development: A Summary of Research Findings. The Elementary School Journal. 100. 443-471. 10.1086/499650.
Shernoff, D. J., Csikszentmihalyi, M., Shneider, B., & Shernoff, E. S. (2003). Student engagement in high school classrooms from the perspective of flow theory. School Psychology Quarterly, 18(2), 158–176. https://doi.org/10.1521/scpq.18.2.158.21860
Wentzel, K. R. (2009). Students' relationships with teachers as motivational contexts. In K. R. Wenzel & A. Wigfield (Eds.), Handbook of motivation at school (pp. 301–322). Routledge/Taylor & Francis Group. https://doi.org/10.4324/9780203879498

SES 27-
Dauber, S., & Epstein, J. L. (1993). Parent attitudes and practices of involvement in inner-city elementary and middle schools. In N. F. Chavkin (Ed.), Families and Schools in a Pluralistic Society (pp. 53–71). Albany, NY: State University of New York Press.
Epstein, J., Sanders, M. et al. (2002). School, Family, and community partnerships—Your handbook for action (2nd ed.). Thousand Oaks, CA: Corwin Press, INC.
Henderson, A. T., & Mapp, K. L. (2002). A new wave of evidence: The impact of school, family, and community connections on student achievement. National Center for Family & Community Connections with Schools.

SES 28-
First addressing students by their name demonstrates respect, captures their attention, and enhances communication, leading to better understanding and engagement.

SES 29-
Battistich, V., Solomon, D., Watson, M., & Schaps, E. (1997). Caring school communities. Educational psychologist, 32(3), 137-151.

SES 30-
Zimmerman, B.J. (2002) Becoming a Self-Regulated Learner: An Overview, Theory Into Practice, 41:2, 64-70, DOI: 10.1207/s15430421tip4102_2

SES 31-
Staff members reinforce a sense of unity and shared commitment to student growth and well-being.

EXECUTIVE FUNCTIONING

EF 1-
Consistency in the learning environment contributes to students' ability to organize tasks, manage time, and complete assignments effectively.

EF 2-
By breaking down larger tasks into manageable components and acknowledging students' efforts along the way, educators support students in effectively managing their tasks and staying motivated toward achieving their goals.

EF 3-
Troia, & Graham, S. (2002). The Effectiveness of a Highly Explicit, Teacher-Directed Strategy Instruction Routine: Changing the Writing Performance of Students with Learning Disabilities. Journal of Learning Disabilities, 35(4), 290–305. https://doi.org/10.1177/00222194020350040101

EF 4-
Dweck, C. S. (2006). Mindset: The new psychology of success. Random House.
Noddings. (2012). The caring relation in teaching. Oxford Review of Education, 38(6), 771–781. https://doi.org/10.1080/03054985.2012.745047

EF 5-
Plass, J.L., Homer, B.D. & Hayward, E.O. Design factors for educationally effective animations and simulations. J Comput High Educ 21, 31–61 (2009). https://doi.org/10.1007/s12528-009-9011-x

EF 6-
Duckworth, Angela & Peterson, Christopher & Matthews, Michael & Kelly, Dennis. (2007). Grit: Perseverance and Passion for Long-Term Goals. Journal of personality and social psychology. 92. 1087-101. 10.1037/0022-3514.92.6.1087.
Dweck, C. S. (2006). Mindset: The new psychology of success. Random House.

EF 7-
Breitwieser, J., Nobbe, L., Biedermann, D., & Brod, G. (2023, August 2). Boosting self-regulated learning with mobile interventions: Planning and prompting help children maintain a regular study routine. Retrieved from osf.io/wqu2c
Zimmerman, B. J. (2002). Becoming a Self-Regulated Learner: An Overview. Theory into Practice, 41, 64-70. http://dx.doi.org/10.1207/s15430421tip4102_2

EF 8-
Breitwieser, J., Nobbe, L., Biedermann, D., & Brod, G. (2023, August 2). Boosting self-regulated learning with mobile interventions: Planning and prompting help children maintain a regular study routine. Retrieved from osf.io/wqu2c
Zimmerman, B. J. (2002). Becoming a Self-Regulated Learner: An Overview. Theory into Practice, 41, 64-70. http://dx.doi.org/10.1207/s15430421tip4102_2

EF 9-
Jensen, Eric, Teaching with the Brain in Mind, 2nd Edition (ASCD, 2nd ed., 2005)
Ratey, J. J., & Hagerman, E. (Collaborator). (2008). Spark: The revolutionary new science of exercise and the brain. Little, Brown and Co.

EF 10-
Neff, K. D. (2003). The development and validation of a scale to measure self-compassion. Self and Identity, 2(3), 223–250. https://doi.org/10.1080/15298860309027

EF 11-
Jennings, P. A., & Greenberg, M. T. (2009). The prosocial classroom: Teacher social and emotional competence in relation to student and classroom outcomes. Review of Educational Research, 79(1), 491–525. https://doi.org/10.3102/0034654308325693
Rimm-Kaufman, Sara & Hamre, Bridget. (2010). The Role of Psychological and Developmental Science in Efforts to Improve Teacher Quality. Teachers College Record. 112. 2988-3023. 10.1177/016146811011201204

EF 12-
Frey N. Hattie J. & Fisher D. (2018). Developing assessment-capable visible learners grades k-12 : maximizing skill will and thrill (First). Corwin Literacy.
Marzano, R. J., Pickering, D. J., & Pollock, J. E. (2001). Classroom instruction that works: Research-based strategies for increasing student achievement. Alexandria, VA: ASCD.

EF 13-
Vock, M., Hollenstein, T., & Perren, S. (2017). Adolescents' daily time management and its associations with feeling of autonomy.Learning and Instruction, 49, 140-149.
Zimmerman, B. J. (2002). Becoming a Self-Regulated Learner: An Overview. Theory into Practice, 41, 64-70. http://dx.doi.org/10.1207/s15430421tip4102_2

EF 14-
Hattie, J. (2012). Visible learning for teachers: Maximizing impact on learning. Routledge/Taylor & Francis Group. https://doi.org/10.4324/9780203181522

EF 15-
Razuk M, Perrin-Fievez F, Gerard CL, Peyre H, Barela JA, Bucci MP. Effect of colored filters on reading capabilities in dyslexic children. Res Dev Disabil. 2018 Dec;83:1-7. doi: 10.1016/j.ridd.2018.07.006. Epub 2018 Jul 23. PMID: 30048864.

Wilkins, A. J., Lewis, E., Smith, F., Rowland, E., & Tweedie, W. (2001). Coloured overlays and their benefit for reading. Journal of Research in Reading, 24(1), 41–64. https://doi.org/10.1111/1467-9817.00132

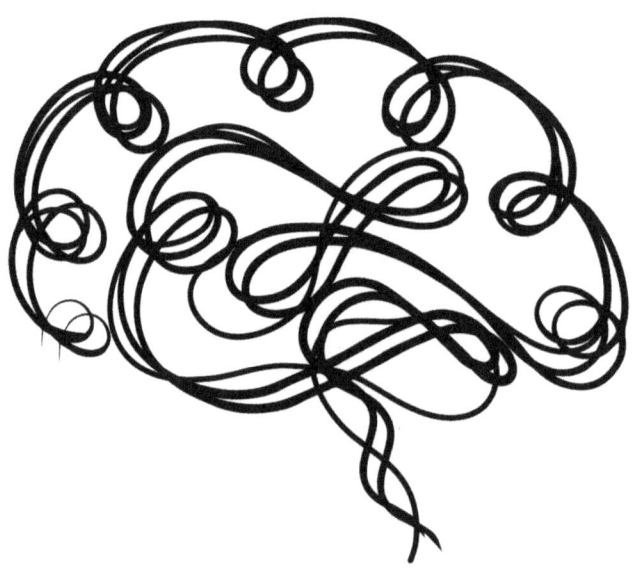

> To live would be an awfully big adventure
> –J.M. Barrie

www.ingramcontent.com/pod-product-compliance
Lightning Source LLC
Chambersburg PA
CBHW080838230426
43665CB00021B/2875